Dramatizing Myths and Tales

Creating Plays for Large Groups

Louise Thistle

Dale Seymour Publications

Dedication

To my artist-teacher friend, Emily Packer, who created the beautiful costumes, props, and art examples for this book, and who has given years of encouragement, inspiration, and support.

Project Editor: Martha Philippa Siegel
Acquisitions Editor: Lois Fowkes
Production/Manufacturing: Leanne Collins
Design Manager: Jeff Kelly
Text Design: Lisa Raine
Cover Design: Rachel Gage
Illustrations: Gail A. Blackmarr, Rachel Gage

This book is published by Dale Seymour Publications, an imprint of
The Alternative Publishing Group of Addison-Wesley Publishing Company.
Copyright © 1995 by Louise Thistle.
Printed in the United States of America.
ORDER NUMBER DS31305
ISBN 0-86651-832-0

1 2 3 4 5 6 7 8 9 10-ML-99 98 97 96 95 94

The author would greatly value feedback from teachers using this material, including information on how the material is used and any other comments or suggestions. Write to her at The Alternative Publishing Group, 200 Middlefield Road, Menlo Park, California 94025.

DALE
SEYMOUR
PUBLICATIONS
P.O. BOX 10888
PALO ALTO, CA 94303

Acknowledgments

I could not have written this book without the guidance, expertise, and help of many people. First, I thank Emily Packer, to whom this book is dedicated.

For help with the African tale, I thank teacher Joyce Kercheval, who shared helpful information on the culture of Ghana which deepened the authenticity of the production. I thank musician-teacher Omar Moore for generously giving me background on African music and instruments. I am deeply indebted to teacher-choreographer Martha Gentry for teaching me the African dance and sharing her knowledge of African theatre and culture.

For help with the Mayan myth, I thank Dr. Alberto Ochoa, Professor of Policy Studies and Cross Cultural Education at San Diego State University, who encouraged me to dramatize a Mayan myth. I am grateful to Marsha Darras, whose fourth graders premiered the myth and who shared with me the students' reactions and follow-up projects.

For guidance on the Japanese tale, I thank child-drama expert and director Sharon Oppenheimer, who provided me with most helpful background and insight into Japanese theatre. Her friendship and expertise is invaluable to me. I am most grateful to the Reverend Dr. Mikel Taxer, who has achieved the rank of Natori in traditional Japanese dance. He taught me the dance steps and provided fascinating information and background on Japanese culture and dance. I also thank teacher Marty Ries, the first to use the Japanese play with high school students. She and her students proved to me the value of using this material to deepen understanding of Japanese culture.

For help with the Native American myth, I thank Richard Bugsbee, Education Specialist for the Museum of Man and member of the Luiseño tribe. He provided me with illuminating information on the symbolism of the steps in the Eagle Power dance. I very much appreciate the help of psychologist-writer Jack Sanford, who introduced me to the Native American tale and showed me its deep significance and value for young people. He also gave me many other invaluable suggestions and ideas.

For help with *Jack and the Beanstalk,* I thank Martha Wild, who shared steps and information on the Morris dance with me. I also thank Jean Stewart, Children's Librarian for the San Diego Public Library and member of Raggle Taggle, a group that performs songs and dances of the British Isles. She suggested steps for the Wake-Up the Spring dance, and continually helped me with research books for the many cultures.

Others I must thank include Rosa Perez, director of Project Excel, a federal grant to develop gifted potential in Hispanic individuals, and director of Project First Step, an intervention program for developing gifted potential among children at an early age. She was the first to see the value of this program for helping develop language, literature understanding, and cultural appreciation in non- and limited-

English speakers as well as other populations. She continues to provide me with many opportunities to dramatize literature in her programs with exceptional teachers.

I thank music teacher Demi McNeil Wallace for many creative sound effect ideas that have opened up a whole musical dimension to these plays. I thank Diane Trigg for the writing try-out idea, found to be so useful by teachers. I am grateful to Emily Dicken, who has generously promoted these programs throughout the country.

I'm very grateful to Susan Longstaff, who uses drama in the Minneapolis Public Schools and who continues to share with me her students' reactions, providing me with many excellent ideas.

I thank Becky Wilkins, who helped design the no-sew tunics and the Mayan headpieces. I am very grateful to Jenny Hartman for her enthusiasm for these projects and her creation of the beautiful, magical atmosphere sticks. Thank you to Dudley Hartman, who has continually provided me with generous help on my computer in times of need.

I thank Salley Deaton for her support, friendship, and particularly for her modeling of excellent, dedicated teaching. I am grateful to Louise Durrant, who rummaged through her library and provided just the books I needed. I thank Deen Schrempf, who has given me beautiful props and instruments.

I deeply appreciate the help of Point Loma Librarian Pat Katka. She has spent hours researching books on drama and the many cultures represented in this book. Her continuous enthusiasm and support is most reinforcing. Thanks to Point Loma Children's Librarian Frieda Pallas for promoting these programs in libraries.

I thank my parents, Lewis Thistle and Josephine Horgan Thistle, who loved acting and who encouraged the development of the imagination. This early nurturing of the imagination and encouragement of "play" stimulated me to do this rewarding work today.

Many creative drama experts have influenced me, but I'm particularly indebted to creative drama pioneer Winifred Ward, who first systematized the dramatizing of stories in the classroom and whose work initially inspired me.

While all of these people have contributed to this book's assets, none are responsible for any lacks, and any errors or omissions are solely my responsibility.

Finally, I thank Charles, who provides a warm, loving, supportive home with our cat, Bell.

Contents

Part II Developing Scripts for Myths and Tales

Introduction

This book fulfills several teacher needs: First, it provides a method for putting on simple, quick, effective plays with groups of up to thirty-five students; second, it provides multicultural dances and plays to help students understand and appreciate other cultures through direct experience; third, it provides material for those with a limited command of the English language to help them learn more about the language in a meaningful way; finally, it provides activities in which students of all levels can learn to work together and, at the same time, grow and develop individually.

In a sense, I started this book when I was a student, when educational-philosopher John Dewey's "learn by doing" approach was popular. I had a teacher who loved drama and involved the class in both informal and stage acting. The experience was exhilarating. It was liberating to act out the strong emotions and lively actions of characters and situations. From then on, drama became my favorite school activity.

Later, as a teacher, I found that students shared this excitement when performing on stage or acting in class. They looked forward to plans, practices, and performances. Indeed, before performances teachers, parents, the principal, and other students shared a little of the excitement. There is something celebratory and magical about theatre that brings the whole school community together and produces memories and commentary for years to come.

As a free-lance drama teacher, I wanted to help teachers direct students in plays. I knew from experience both the joys and problems teachers encounter when trying to stage a class play using traditional scripts and production styles. I had to solve the problem of line memorization, in which students do not learn their lines until the last moment, if at all; the problem of backstage fooling around; the problem of uneven roles, with three or four major roles and any number of insignificant walk-ons; and the problem of needing to create elaborate costumes and scenery. Eliminating these problems enables teachers to focus on student enjoyment and participation, and to concentrate on the development of students' imagination and their theater and performance skills. The solution to these problems is *narrative mime theatre.*

Eliminating Line Memorization

Most scripts require that students memorize lines—sometimes quite a few of them. However, students often do not learn these lines until the last moment, and some are still shaky on performance day.

The essence of good acting is to get inside the characters and portray them truthfully rather than simply to memorize lines. Students who pursue acting will certainly need to memorize lines, but this should not be the emphasis for beginners. Development of imagination and characterization skills is of greater concern at the beginning level.

Line memorization is virtually eliminated with narrative mime theatre by using storytellers who read from scripts. The actors' lines spring directly from strong cues given by the storytellers. For example, a storyteller reads "Jack's mother was worried," and the mother's line is "I'm so worried." Using storytellers has an immediate creative benefit, too. Actors never hold a script. They can move around freely and act the character completely, with their whole bodies.

Eliminating Backstage Fooling Around

A teacher who has directed one play may never want to direct another because of backstage fooling around. Most plays require that characters enter and exit from backstage, so the problem is virtually unavoidable. Lecturing students to pipe down backstage is time-consuming and exhausting. In addition, students who are goofing around backstage are not out front listening and learning to act by watching other students during rehearsal.

In narrative mime, the solution is to have all actors sit on the stage at all times, in chairs arranged in a semicircle in view of the audience and director. The costumes and props they use for their parts are under their chairs. The storytellers stand on either side of the stage, and a sound crew with rhythm instruments for sound effects laid out before them sit at a table to one side.

Having the performers out front enables the audience to see the theatrics. The audience watches a student on the sound crew tap a wood block as a dog trots along, and sees students wiggle blue fabric and ring bells to create a rippling lake.

Eliminating the Star System

Most scripts feature a few leading roles and relegate the rest of the participants to walk-ons as villagers or to props such as trees. Naturally the trees and villagers often become bored and restless. The goal in narrative mime presentations is for all students to have significant roles in order to feel involved, to learn theatre, and to practice performance skills. Not all students want leading roles of course, and some prefer not to act at all. The non-actors comprise a sound crew of six. Each member is assigned several rhythm instruments or the piano to create sound effects that enhance the action and help the actors act with more conviction. For example, a sound crew shakes rattles to create the illusion of swirling smoke and rings bells to help actors fly more lightly like birds.

Students in narrative mime theatre who want to act but do not want a major role portray inanimate objects using props and movement, such as dancing flames or mountain peaks. Students playing these roles are assigned several parts, keeping them active and involved throughout the play. Roles are often played in pairs or threes to loosen inhibitions and increase the fluidity of creative expression.

A bonus of incorporating sound effects and inanimate objects is that it guarantees a production's success. So much activity is occurring on stage in a narrative mime performance—both visual and auditory stimuli—that imperfections are overlooked.

Eliminating Elaborate Costumes and Scenery

Sets and elaborate costumes can be time-consuming to create and can detract from what is most important—developing the imagination and learning acting and performance skills. So much time is spent on sets and costumes in traditional productions that the central skills which are the essence of good performing suffer. Students should realize that acting is created by performers through their use of voice and movement rather than by elaborate costumes. It is better to play a part with conviction but without a costume than to play it limply in an elaborate one.

In narrative mime theatre, performers wear all-black clothing to create uniformity. Costume pieces (mostly hats and other head pieces) and fabrics and simple props are kept under the actors' chairs so that they can be popped on or picked up when needed to act out a part. Scenery can continually move and change. Students comprise the set, and their simple costumes and props transform them from one piece of scenery into another, challenging the imagination of the performers and audience alike.

Teaching Acting Skills

Teachers often find that students act woodenly when they perform on stage. To eliminate wooden acting, characters in narrative mime presentations are given specific actions in almost every sentence: "the chief glared," or the weaver "threw up her hands in fright," or the snake "hissed and slithered." These actions require the students' attention and participation; they give students something specific to do.

The Value of Dramatizing Multicultural Tales and Myths

I began this project to provide students with multicultural stories to dramatize. As I field-tested the material, I grew more and more excited. I discovered that embodying a culture's rituals and customs serves to enhance understanding of and deepen appreciation for its unique qualities.

Psychologists talk about two kinds of knowledge: one is intellectual knowledge, gained through activities such as reading and discussion; another is knowledge gained through direct experience. Knowledge about another culture may be best gained by coupling direct experience with reading and discussion.

Dramatizing stories and rituals enables students to experience the genius of a culture, the qualities unique to that culture. Students cannot be passive and uninvolved as they complete a Shinto bow, mime eating from a small rice bowl with chopsticks, or pretend to dig a furrow. These acting experiences teach students new techniques and ways of expressing themselves as actors, while expanding and enriching their dimensions as human beings.

Using *Dramatizing Myths and Tales* in the Classroom

Chapter One explains how to produce the plays presented in this book, with detailed information on the mechanics of directing these and other plays. It includes casting, stage blocking, acting methods, and techniques for training the sound crew and storytellers.

Chapter Two provides guidelines for making or obtaining simple, generic costumes that can be used for a variety of different plays, and explains how to create rhythm instruments from objects found around home or school.

Chapter Three suggests a step-by-step rehearsal schedule, from introducing the play through after-performance follow-ups. The activities outlined in this chapter may be used in conjunction with the acting exercises specific to each script.

Chapter Four provides guidelines for dramatizing the plays informally in the classroom using two different techniques. These techniques may be used to explore further characterization and creative development, to provide more practice and training in narrative mime, to vary rehearsals prior to an audience presentation, or to provide students with a simple dramatic experience for the classroom only.

Part Two presents scripts for five multicultural myths and tales to act. They are *Talk, Talk, Talk* (West African); *The Creation and the Birth of the Corn God* (Mayan); *Coyote and the Swallowing Monster* (Native North American Indian); *The Crane Maiden* (Japanese); and *Jack and the Beanstalk* (British). These plays have been field-tested and performed in grades three through twelve with great success. The scripts are set off from the rest of the book by decorative borders, one to define each myth or tale. The scripts may easily be photocopied and distributed to each student participating in a production. Please note that permission is granted for photocopying the *scripts only* for your class alone, and that such permission is granted for productions in which an admission fee is not charged. For all other uses, written permission must be obtained from the author.

Each play emphasizes the particular customs and rituals of the culture depicted, highlighting its theater-performance rituals and conventions. For example, the West African tale uses drumming and chanting with communal movement, while the Japanese play focuses on the expression of powerful emotions in highly stylized poses.

To help students become fully involved and to help them better understand and appreciate the culture depicted, chapters include background information and questions on the story itself, the culture, and the theater-performance conventions of the culture. Research activities and activities to compare and contrast the story and culture with others in the book are also included.

Chapters also include acting and performance activities to do at rehearsals to get students involved in the characters and to teach them how to act, tell stories, and perform sound effects. Each chapter describes how to perform a simple dance of the culture and suggests appropriate music to accompany it. Finally, the chapters describe simple costume pieces, fabrics, and props that can be used.

Your experience with narrative mime theatre should not be limited to the scripts presented in this book. Chapter Ten describes how to begin developing your own narrative mime script based on stories chosen for their relevance to your specific teaching situation. Students in groups can write, direct, and produce their own narrative mime scripts based on myths or folk tales, and instructions for guiding such activities are provided as well.

Now more than ever, students need a creative vent for strong feelings. They crave ways to develop and use their imaginations, the source of all creativity. They need and want to enact the powerful characters and situations which lurk in their imaginations, bigger than life.

The theatre is bigger than life. Performing in a play is a memorable occasion, and students are likely to never forget the experience. Everyone needs and craves bigger-than-life experiences and the richness, vitality, and excitement such experiences provide. Helping students to experience these feelings—along with the well-deserved applause that accompanies such efforts—is a gratifying experience, building confidence for individual students and a feeling of team spirit and group pride among the class.

PART ONE

Getting Started

CHAPTER ONE

The Mechanics of Producing and Directing a Play

The plays in this book can easily be produced in two weeks. Schedule daily rehearsals of about an hour in classrooms of up to thirty-five students. No drama experience is necessary. Each play takes about twenty-five minutes to perform.

The plays use a narrative mime and dialogue to act each story. The scripts can be photocopied from this book and distributed to each performer. In this narrative mime theatre, four narrators (storytellers) position themselves on the stage, two on each side, and read from the scripts. The actors, dressed in black, sit in chairs in a semicircle on stage. Their simple costume pieces, props, and fabrics to create scenery are under their chairs or on their laps.

When the storytellers read the story, the actors have their props ready and stand to act their parts as the narrator describes the action. For example, when a storyteller reads, "A dog trotted along," the actor wearing dog ears stands up from the chair and trots onto the stage. All actors' lines and actions are derived from strong cues given by the storytellers.

A sound crew of six, all dressed in black, sits at a table or piano beside the stage with rhythm instruments or homemade instruments laid out before them to create sound effects. (The piano player need not know how to play the piano.) The table and piano are placed so that the crew can see the actors and the audience can watch the sound effects being made. (See diagram.) All of the sound cues are in the script read by the storytellers.

Stage Layout

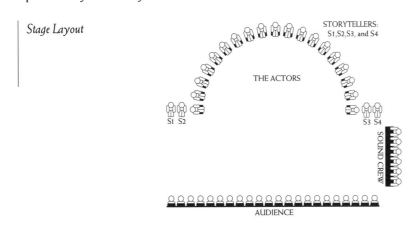

All scripts are accompanied by self-explanatory acting activities that can be used as warm-up exercises to begin rehearsals. The activities help students develop their imaginations, get involved with the characters, and learn to act. Play chapters also include background information and questions on each story, focusing on the culture and theater-performance rituals and techniques to deepen students' appreciation and understanding. The activities can be used before rehearsals, during rehearsals, and after the performance, depending on students' needs.

Production Notes for each script suggest costume pieces and rhythm instruments that can be used. Steps for a simple dance and music to accompany it are also provided.

This chapter describes techniques that may be used to cast, direct, and produce each play with students of varying abilities. It also outlines ways to involve the audience in order to obtain helpful feedback for the performers. This involvement deepens audience understanding of and appreciation for the theater-performance skills necessary to create a production.

The following techniques may be used to train performers and direct the plays in this book, as well as any narrative mime scripts you develop on your own. Tips for teaching the dance steps, creating costumes, and involving the audience are also provided. A step-by-step rehearsal schedule incorporating these techniques is outlined in Chapter Three.

The Style of These Plays

The characters in the plays presented here are types—the domineering chief; the graceful, elegant maiden; the powerful, regal Moon Goddess; the quivering mouse. Gestures and movements used to portray these types must be clear and enlarged. Each character, therefore, must have a distinctive vocal and movement style. Each must also find a physical stance for clear and immediate identification and representation. For example, the chief in the African play should have a domineering voice and stance, and the delicate crane in the Japanese play should have a light voice and lyrical, graceful wing flapping.

The style of these and all narrative mime plays is presentational; the characters primarily present the story directly to the audience. It differs from realism, in which the actors speak and relate only to each other as if the audience does not exist. In presentational theatre, the actors open up in a three-quarter ballet-style position. They turn and speak to the audience, frequently pantomiming actions and exaggerating facial expressions. Actions, gestures, and characterizations are enlarged.

Students need not know the term *presentational.* They should know, however, that they need to open up their bodies and play lines to the audience. Blocking techniques to achieve this are in the step-by-step rehearsal guide.

Theatre of the Imagination

The plays in this book emphasize the development and use of the imagination. Visual interpretations of characters and objects are presented as they are described by the storytellers or other actors. Blue fabric is rippled to form a lake, arms join to form the peaked roof of a cottage, characters made of wood walk stiffly across the stage.

Sound effects are executed in full view, serving to enhance the action and, at times, add to the rhythm, lyricism, and humor of the play. This type of presentation demands that both the actors and the audience use their imagination to fill in the details and bring the characters and action to life.

The Director's Roles

The Director as Leader

The director's first job is to lead, so they must be very organized and know what their goals are for every rehearsal. It is helpful to communicate these goals and the procedure that will be followed to achieve them at the beginning of the rehearsal so that everyone is clear on what will happen. Performers feel a sense of security and purpose if they know what they are aiming for. The step-by-step rehearsal guide suggests goals for each session.

The Director as Reinforcer

Everyone needs praise. Young beginning performers need lots of encouragement to reinforce their efforts. The need is understandable. It takes courage to go before an audience. Some students feel vulnerable when they expose their imaginations and themselves in such a direct, physical way, and the experience is new. In addition, the creative process is delicate. Support will help beginning artists develop their talents and gain self-confidence so that they will hunger to do more.

It is most beneficial to begin every rehearsal by mentioning what students have done well. Focus on anything that is contributing to the endeavor and to the development of their imaginations. Compliment students on how well they are working as a team, how attentive they are, how much you appreciate their enthusiasm, or how impressed you are by their use of their imaginations and willingness to jump into the acting activities so wholeheartedly. This general reinforcement will go a long way toward making students feel as though they comprise a successful, creative team and committing them to and involving them in the production.

An effective way to get students involved is to ask them what they think might be done to improve the production, encouraging them to articulate what is needed for a good production. It shows them that you appreciate their insights, but perhaps most important, students tend to be eager and willing to push for certain improvements that are their own ideas. Students often listen to each others' ideas with more enthusiasm and interest than they would have for ideas expressed by the director.

The Director as Coach

While encouraging students to participate, the director must act like an athletic coach and push students to improve. This direct exhortation is essential in getting students to fulfill technical requirements such as speaking louder, creating clear, emphatic gestures, and using enthusiasm throughout rehearsals.

Performers respond well to an assertive director just as athletes do to a coach who buoys them up and pushes them to achieve their best. This approach should, of course, be coupled with hearty praise for improvement and effort.

The Director as Artistic Collaborator

Perhaps the most productive and fulfilling aspect of putting on a production for both the performers and the director is to reinforce, encourage, and use students' creative ideas and input whenever possible.

Students become excited and heavily committed to a production when their ideas are highlighted, honored, and used. It fosters a feeling of creative empowerment and gives students confidence to risk offering more ideas. Students often have a fresh perspective and come up with highly imaginative ideas that enrich the production. For example, a director of *Talk, Talk, Talk* felt that the production lost its liveliness when the characters repeated over and over the different things that talked to them. A student suggested having the things themselves pop up and repeat what they had said each time, an ingenious solution that made the production much livelier and more dramatic.

Naturally the director has the final say on what to include, and not all ideas are feasible or beneficial. If an idea cannot be used, showing appreciation for it and explaining why it is not right for the production is appreciated and understood. For example, if someone suggests wearing full costumes, explain that theatre of the imagination focuses on acting and the use of the imagination rather than an elaborate wardrobe.

Finding Creative Solutions to Performance Problems

Directors face a universal dilemma: becoming frustrated if performers do not do what the part requires. It is a temptation to hammer away at the actor to get him or her to "do it right." This, of course, can be counterproductive for everyone concerned. Indeed, performances do not improve under pressure, and students may lose enthusiasm for the project.

Creative solutions can often be found for acting or performance problems. If a performer is not doing what you request after several tries, it is usually best just to skip it and continue with the rehearsal. A solution may be found later, or the problem may resolve itself. The student may not really want to play the part, a possibility that can be discussed later. If a character cannot speak loudly enough, you might decide to cut some dialogue to make the role easier.

Avoiding the Burden of Perfectionism

Many directors of beginners feel hassled, especially as the performance time nears. The production method for these plays is designed to avoid much of the harried-director syndrome by eliminating most line memorization and by having so much going on that if one thing does not work perfectly, something else will compensate for it.

A way to avoid the burden of perfectionism is to keep your primary goal in mind at all times. If the goal for these beginners is that they first and foremost enjoy the experience so that they will want to do more, learn about other cultures through direct experience, and learn theater and acting skills, the burden of perfectionism can be lifted.

Perfection is not possible, nor is it desirable. Perfection can be stultifying, hindering spontaneity and the creative process. Instead, give students two distinct goals.

First, have them focus on playing their role to the best of their ability. For example, if playing a barking dog, they should snarl and bark with their whole voice and body; if playing a storyteller, they should speak in a way to excite and enthuse the audience; if playing a sound crew member, they must pay attention in order to play the effect appropriately and on cue. Second, have students work as a team and be ready to help each other out when problems occur. Giving students these two clear goals can help reduce self-consciousness and stage fright by helping them know where to focus their attention.

Three Principles of Good Acting

There are three simple principles that students should follow in order to act convincingly and with style:

- Believe in the part you are playing.
- Use your voice and movements expressively to portray characters and their feelings.
- Exercise control over your emotions and actions.

These principles provide the foundation; they are followed by all good actors. If students follow them, their acting will be successful and they will communicate with the audience. Otherwise, their acting will not be effective nor will the experience be worthwhile.

To train students in the principles, it helps to list them on a chart and discuss each one individually. The warm-up activities included with each script enable students to practice each principle. You might also use suggestions from my book *Dramatizing Aesop's Fables* (Dale Seymour Publications, 1993) to practice the acting principles informally in the classroom. Specific guidelines are given below.

Believing

Believing is the most important principle. If students are able to make believe that they are the parts they are playing, they are well on the way to executing the other principles successfully as well.

Discuss what it means for actors to believe or pretend they are the characters they are playing in order for the performance to seem real. Ask how the audience would feel if someone playing a powerful character shuffled onto the stage and mumbled his or her lines. Model contrasting ways that characters can be played, convincingly and not so convincingly. Continue by conducting warm-up activities provided with each script.

Voice and Movement

Ask students what it means for actors to use their voices and movements to show who the characters are and what they are feeling. Discuss ways in which voices and bodies are the actors' tools. To model the concept of using the voice, say the word *voice* twice, first as a powerful giant and then as a tiny mouse voice. Then say the word *movement* twice, first assuming a giant's stance and then cowering and shivering as a timorous mouse. Then have students do a voice and movement activity.

Control

Ask students what it means for actors to have control over their movements and voices to make the performance artistic and keep it from becoming chaotic. Ask what might happen if dancers leaping on stage were to go out of control. Perhaps model examples of controlled movement and not-so controlled movement.

Have students practice one of the script's control activities, such as slow motion movement, running in place, or creating a frozen picture to express powerful emotions. Reinforce good control and artistic form.

Stage Acting Techniques

There are several acting techniques for narrative mime theatre that may be used to improve students' performance skills and enhance the quality of the production.

Finding a Character Stance

Each character needs a particular stance that communicates clearly to the audience at every moment of the play exactly who that character is. For example, the Moon Goddess must look powerful and royal; she might stand erect, with head slightly up and arms quietly by her side. Tricky Coyote might lean over alertly, paws up, showing his eagerness. The delicate Crane might stand with feet in an open ballet position with wings slightly raised by her side.

The character stance is most important when the actor is waiting on stage for a cue or listening to another character act a role. Students should assume their character stance positions whenever they are not involved in an action. Otherwise they tend to stand like themselves or fidget. You will likely need to give students a stance to take; most students do not develop one naturally. Another option is to have students assume a neutral stance when they are not acting, standing completely still with hands next to their sides, but this is hard for most of them to do.

Miming

Because the plays use no scenery, the audience depends on actors to pretend that specific objects exist and are being manipulated. To mime successfully, actors must envision that the object is there and that they are using it. For example, Jack must see the big piece of crusty French bread on the plate. He must pick it up to relieve his hunger and rip into it with his teeth.

To mime for the stage, essential details are exaggerated and emphasized so that they are clearly communicated. For example, the Moon Goddess sees a clump of wet gray clay on the ground, picks it up, feels the texture to see if she can use it. She carefully forms a person's head and makes eyes, mouth, and nose in such a way that her actions are understood. Mime activities are provided in the scripts.

Gesturing

The scripts need dramatic gestures because the style is larger than life, and dramatic gestures will make a story and its characters come alive. Storytellers include gestures as they read. For example, if something is icy, the storyteller might shiver. Gestures heighten speeches and excite the audience.

Actors need gestures too, especially at points where there is little action in the play. For example, when the Moon Goddess calls for Earth to form, there is no written action, but a big circular gesture can beckon Earth to come. Encourage students to add as many appropriate gestures as possible in order to involve the audience and make the action come to life.

Acting Inanimate Objects

Playing inanimate objects can develop the imagination more than any other aspect of performing narrative mime plays. It also makes the literature come fully alive. The following tips will help students play objects:

- Students should have props or fabrics ready to use so they will be able to create the object instantaneously.
- Students should portray the object's quality. For example, if mist swirls, students might whirl fabric ribbons gracefully with flowing motions to create the illusion of airy mist.
- Students should act only when storytellers cue them. For example, when storytellers say, "the lake rippled," actors ripple the cloth. However, when the narration resumes, students should stop rippling so that all attention is on the next action.
- Students should sit when action is over or freeze waiting for their next cue.

Character Motivation

Understanding why a character is behaving in a certain way will help enhance the actor's portrayal. All actions are done for a reason or purpose, so each character's motivation is clear and immediate. For example, the farmer in *Talk, Talk, Talk* runs because he feels he is being haunted by talking things. The crane in *The Crane Maiden* pushes off from the ground and flaps her wings strongly to prevent being caught or trapped. Understanding motivation will also help actors remember their stage blocking or movement because their actions have a purpose. The stronger and more pressing the purpose, the more the actor will feel compelled to perform the action and get involved in the part. For example, the chief in the African tale tells the villagers to leave or they will be arrested because he fears their talk might cause havoc throughout the village. If the actor knows this is the chief's motivation, the part will be played with more conviction.

Even the storytellers have a motivation: to convince the audience that this is the most fascinating story they have ever heard. Focusing on this motivation will help the storytellers speak clearly and with enthusiasm.

Putting Yourself in the Shoes, Fur, or Feathers of a Character—The "Magic If"

The great Russian director Stanislavski created and developed an acting method called the "magic if." An actor considers "what if" I were in this character's circumstance, what would I do, how would I feel, or how would I act? To do this, it helps if students can visualize themselves in the situation. The more they are able to climb into the situation of the character, the more meaningful and authentic their acting will be. The director can help by painting a vivid picture of the situation.

For example, a student becoming the crane caught in a trap would try to imagine how it would feel to have a leg clamped in the jaws of a steel trap, and would react to that feeling. An actor pretending to be an old man wearing heavy boots and trudging through heavy snow would try to experience how it would feel to be that character. Some of the acting exercises provided in this book help students experience the characters' situations by identifying with them.

Three Principles of Good Storytelling

The role of storytellers is to excite and involve the audience in the story. They should follow three vocal principles:

- Projection, or speaking loudly enough so that everyone can hear;
- Diction, or saying each sound or syllable clearly so that the audience knows precisely what each word is;
- Colorization, or coloring speech so that words sound like what they describe— for example, *icy* sounds icy, and *hot* sounds hot.

List the vocal principles on a chart and emphasize them during rehearsals. A way to warm up voices and get punch into speech is to take a section of a play and say it line by line, following the principles and having students echo you.

Helpful Storytelling Hints

The following points will enhance the storytellers' roles:

- Students should make their voices go up at the end of sentences so that the last word, which is often the most important, has brightness and is not swallowed.
- Students should emphasize the most important words in each sentence.
- Storytellers should mark their parts with a highlighting pen and follow along with a finger; a frequent storyteller flaw is not coming in on cue and creating dead spots or lulls between narration.

Training the Sound Crew

Audiences frequently say that their favorite part of a show is the sound effects. Making sound effects develops musical and auditory discrimination skills and adds another theatrical element to the performance.

Several elements are required for creating effective sound effects:

- Come in on cue. Students should highlight their parts and get instruments ready ahead of time.
- Capture the quality of the sound being imitated. For example, when the Giant stomps on, the drum is thumped to imitate the heavy, plodding step; when a river ripples, a bell tinkles to simulate the rippling sound. Some students can instinctively create accurate sound qualities. Others need some modeling.
- Capture the theatrical clarity and brightness of the effects by playing them crisply and emphatically. The sound must communicate artistically to the audience. For example, the wood block should be tapped neatly as Coyote trots and the bells should be rung with a lively brightness for the sparkling lake.

- Do not rush. To ensure that enough time is taken to create particular effects, have students count to ten slowly when appropriate. The sound effects coupled with the moving scenery pieces are a show highlight.

Students will enjoy thinking up their own effects and will want to include as many as possible. Naturally this should be encouraged as long as the effect contributes to the production.

To encourage inventive ideas, let students try out any effects that come to mind during the rehearsals and then tell them on the spot whether each effect will work or not. In this way students will learn that art is a process of trial and error and that artists have many ideas, some that can be used and some that cannot.

Performing the Dances

The audience and performers enjoy performing or watching students do the ethnic dances included in this book. Dances are individual, unique expressions of cultures. They also bond a group and develop a sense of community, much as in the cultures where they were created. It is liberating and therapeutic to act with the whole body. Dancing also teaches through experience the unique characteristics of a culture. For example, African dances often have an improvisational style using every part of the body; Japanese dances strike formal, sculptured poses.

Each script describes how to do a cultural dance to begin and end each play. Dances are intentionally simplified so that anyone can do them. The following suggestions will help you teach the ethnic dances in this book:

- Make sure students know the purpose of the dance, which is given in each dance description, so they know what they are aiming for.
- Use authentic music of each culture.
- Choose a natural dancer as a leader. The leader provides central organization by initiating new moves and directing the action. The leader's style will influence the other dancers.

Casting

There are many ways to cast a play and thoughtful casting is the most important element of a successful production. Minimal line memorization greatly enhances the possibility of getting the right student in the right part. If a student is miscast, cannot handle the part, or is absent, another can easily take the role even on the day of performance.

Explain the concept of flexible casting so that students know what to expect. Avoid hurt feelings for students who are trying but are unable to handle a big part by giving them several small roles to act.

Three methods of casting a play are given below. Using more than one method is a good idea so that you can see students in different situations and gauge their involvement, ability, and commitment. Regardless of what method is used, keep the casting flexible so that students' parts may be changed.

The Improvisational Tryout

For an improvisational tryout, have students do some of the acting activities given with the scripts and observe how they respond. You will see who has the most natural acting ability and who is most interested and involved. Those who perform with little commitment may not respond to acting and may need to build confidence by playing a small part.

The Written Tryout

The written tryout helps students articulate what the characters are like and shows their commitment to and involvement in the production. It also makes them think about how they might perform a role. For the written tryout, follow the steps below:

- Have students list three roles they want to play in order of preference (roles include acting, storytelling, and sound crew).
- Have students describe what the characters are like or, in the case of storytellers or sound crew, what is required to play the role effectively.
- Have students explain why they should be chosen to play the role.

Evaluate these responses and consider them.

The Formal Tryout

For the formal tryout, you choose parts of the script for students to read aloud, and they go to the front of the room or stage and try out for the roles they want. This method allows you to focus on each individual and see how students compare with each other. Rate students according to voice projection and characterization, essential requirements for leading actors and storytellers.

Spotting the Born Actor

There is such a thing as a born actor. The born actor is able to jump inside and express the feelings of many characters. Born actors are also hungry to act. The best of them will listen eagerly to and even solicit the director's ideas and then try to do them because they are anxious to improve.

Born actors come up with many of their own ideas for parts and do them spontaneously during rehearsals or ask the director if they can do them. These students often have strong voices and expressive bodies. They are comfortable on stage. Not all born actors will have all of these traits in equal degree, but they will have most of them.

For a performance to please an audience, it is often helpful to put the most competent actors in leading roles. Some might argue that leading roles should be spread out democratically, and for classroom dramatizations this is a good idea. When performing before an audience, however, both the students and the audience will feel more comfortable if a strong actor who is able and eager to handle the part is in the biggest role. The strong actor will improve the production and will inspire others by example. Their confidence will put more timid students at ease. These strong actors should be encouraged to work with other students to share their acting ideas and techniques, thus creating an atmosphere of cooperative learning.

Occasionally two or three students are nearly equally good actors. If in doubt, choose the most responsible student with the strongest voice for the most important role. It is essential that an actor be heard. Of course, a student who is reliable, follows directions, and gives 100% effort will improve over time.

If all contenders fit this criteria, then you will have to choose one. Perhaps mention that at one time or another every excellent actor has had the experience of not getting a desired role. Indeed, their success is due to hard work and persistence despite setbacks and adversity.

Blocking

One of the director's most important functions is to give actors their blocking or stage movements. Good blocking enables everyone in the audience to see everything that is going on. It also helps to tell the story clearly and lends variety and dramatic interest to the production.

To help describe the blocking to actors, the stage is divided into areas. (See diagram.) Some areas get more attention than others. For example, standing center stage naturally gets more attention than standing upstage left. Downstage areas are often strong because they are close to the audience. Characters usually talk to the audience from downstage.

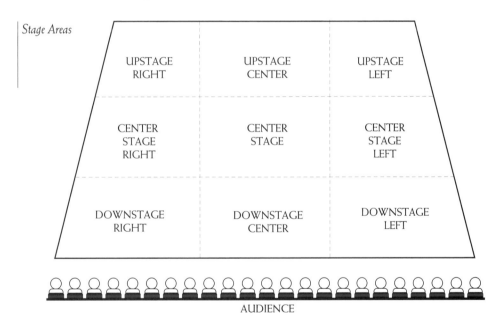

The term upstage dates back to a time when stages were *raked* or sloped upward. The area opposite upstage is downstage. Stage right and left are identified from the actors' point of view. As mentioned, some areas are stronger than others, though it is best to use every stage area, even the corners, to open up the stage's full potential and to keep the action from looking cramped or cluttered.

To help students learn the areas, draw the diagram on chart paper or the chalkboard, discuss it, and have students practice moving to the various areas in the front of the classroom or on stage. The word *stage* need not be used when giving the directions: "Go up right" or "Move down left."

There are two blocking techniques students need to practice to share the play with an audience:

- Open up to the audience.
- Don't get blocked.

Ideas for teaching these techniques are described below.

Invite a student to the front of the room and discuss a topic such as the weather. Stand in profile. Then, open up your body in a three-quarter position as you talk, so that most of your face and body is visible to everyone. Ask which position is better to share the dialogue with the whole audience. You may wish to compare body language during a conversation in life to that used during a dialogue in the theater.

Ask another student to come to the front of the room. Begin the conversation, this time standing directly in front of the student. Ask what actors might do if they find themselves in this situation on stage. An obvious answer is to step aside so that you are not blocked. Another is to step back so that the other actor must also step back in order to talk to you.

Check the Sightlines

Sometimes at performances, directors go to a side of the auditorium and realize that the audience cannot see what is going on from that viewpoint. To prevent this from happening, view the whole play from all parts of the audience during rehearsals.

Focus on the Important Action

The blocking must help tell the story accurately, so the audience focuses its attention on the most important action occurring on the stage at any given time. The action may involve a character or a prop. Use the following guidelines and techniques to block the action:

- Place the important character or action at center stage or in some other strong spot.
- Create a frozen picture of the character or the situation.
- Situate the most important action on a higher plane than others by having the character stand on a box, extend his or her arms high in the air, and so on.
- Have other characters turn and perhaps even point at the central character.
- Make sure that a new, important entering character goes to center stage or some other strong area so that she or he is not lost in the background.

Create Variety and Dramatic Interest

Blocking should be varied and have dramatic and theatrical interest. Remember to use every area of the stage to open up the action and use the stage's full potential.

Students on their own will not usually use the corners of the stage, so just send them there. This is especially necessary in scenes with group actions such as birds flying. Students tend to cluster close together, perhaps due to nervousness.

A simple, effective way to create variety and interesting stage pictures is to place students at different levels by having some lie down, some sit, some kneel on one knee, some kneel on both knees, some stand bent over, some stand erect with hands up, and so on.

The inanimate objects in particular should be placed on different levels to create attractive stage pictures. For example, the lake actors might kneel as they shimmer the lake cloth. Berry bushes might stand, sit, and kneel to create a variety of heights.

Pacing

To be dramatic, a play must build in intensity. The most dramatic incident, of course, happens near the end. A production may be boring if the actors do the same actions at the same level of intensity throughout the play.

For example, in *Talk, Talk, Talk* the characters get excited when objects speak to them. Each time an object speaks the actors run away. The farmer and other characters must get progressively more excited during the story as more and more things talk at them. The director must find a method to show this building excitement and intensity. One example might be for the characters to run with their arms held low. Each time another thing talks, their arms and running motions might get higher and more exaggerated and their voices might increase in pitch.

The Professional Curtain Call

The curtain call ends the show and is the last impression the audience has of the performance. It should be professional and have panache. A well-staged curtain call makes students feel professional, too, and can influence their whole attitude toward the performance. The techniques of presenting oneself in a curtain call can transfer to other public situations in which a confident, professional stance is required. We all need an effective public persona at times in order to be a success.

Have a leader, Storyteller One, conduct the proceedings by announcing each group of performers individually. Begin with the actors, then identify the sound crew, and finally the storytellers.

When each group of performers is called, they stand, step forward, say their names loudly and clearly, and remain standing. Storyteller One gives his or her own name last. When all are standing, Storyteller One turns and faces them and lifts his or her hands up in the air. All performers do this, too, and when the storyteller's hands are lowered and he or she bows, they do the same and then sit.

A frequent flaw is that students say their names too softly. Insist that they say their names loudly, like a cheer. Most want to speak up—they just need a little encouragement. Point out that they deserve to cheer their names because they have done an excellent job. Practice the curtain call several times, explaining its importance in ensuring that the performance concludes with energy and style.

Involving the Audience

A pre- and post-performance discussion and feedback evaluation of the play will increase audience enthusiasm, teach the audience performance techniques, and provide the performers with much-appreciated feedback. It also shows the audience that they have a valued and respected role.

Prior to the performance, explain to the audience a little about the play they will be seeing. This might include mention of some prominent cultural feature, such as the corn dance in the Mayan play.

Tell the audience that the performers want their feedback. Ask them to observe how the actors make believe and use their voices and bodies to portray the characters. Give them examples of special features to watch for. Ask them to watch the storytellers to see what they do with their voices and movements to make the story come alive. Ask them to listen to how the sound crew makes sound effects to go with the actions.

After the performance, ask the audience for comments. Make sure all performance elements are mentioned by asking questions as necessary. The audience might also draw a picture or write the performers letters describing what they liked.

Performer's Reflection

Teachers often mention that a play production is one of the year's highlights. Students are naturally excited and buoyed up after the experience. A follow-up reflection helps students articulate what the experience meant to them. It is also a helpful, calming transition to the daily business of the classroom.

Some possible reflection questions include the following:

- What did you enjoy most about doing this play?
- What was the most difficult part of the play for you?
- What was your reaction to having an audience?
- Would you like to do another drama project? Why or why not? If yes, what might it be?

Students might also make a class album describing and drawing their favorite part of the performance.

CHAPTER TWO

Setting the Scene

In dramatizing narrative mime plays for theatre of the imagination, it is important to create an atmosphere of vibrancy and excitement. Choosing appropriate costumes, props and musical instruments for the performers—whether hand-made or store-bought—is a critical step in this process.

Costumes and Fabrics

People's eyes light up when they see costumes. There is something magical about seeing the beautiful colors and textures. Simple pieces can be more exciting than full costumes because they demand that the audience use its imagination to fill in the gaps. For example, creating a monster's heart by opening and closing a red umbrella with a heart drawn on it delights the audience because of its imaginative use of a familiar object. A green feather boa waved to represent a palm tree is both innovative and intriguing.

Minimal costume pieces also help students develop their imaginations; their offbeat quality frees students to become more uninhibited, and even the simplest costume piece allows students to become different characters. The costume need not look exactly like what it represents; it can be symbolic—a yellow visor can be a bird's bill, a green cape can be a tree.

Incorporating Costumes

Tips for incorporating costume pieces are given below. Specific costume suggestions are included with each play. The *Bibliography* at the end of this book suggests additional sources of information on creating simple costumes.

- Keep the costume pieces simple; the most theatrical piece can be the easiest to make or obtain. For example, aqua nylon fabric rippled makes a beautiful lake. Red store-bought headbands and a white cape create a striking crane.
- Make sure the costumes are easy to put on and take off.
- Keep scenery fabrics light and small so that they are easy to manipulate and store under chairs.
- Observe how a fabric or costume looks from a distance.

- Strive to create ethnic costumes but keep them dynamic and do not sacrifice theatricality for authenticity. Use, when possible, a few artifacts from the culture, such as a Japanese dance fan or African hat, to stimulate believability and heighten interest.
- Aim for simplicity of color and design rather than complexity and busy fabrics. Bright, clear colors appeal to the young and are generally right for these plays.
- Do not repeat the same costume piece for different characters in the same production. For example, if there are two different birds in different scenes, give each bird a different costume. You might use an orange visor for one and a yellow visor for the other.
- Seek help from parents. This will take the burden off of you and can stimulate creativity. Observing the homemade costumes at Halloween can provide many inventive costuming ideas.

Collecting Costume Pieces and Props

It is exciting to find a prop or beautiful fabric or costume piece that is just right for one play or might be used for another. Props often inspire the addition of another character. For example, find a neat feather hat and maybe add another bird.

Thrift stores, garage sales, parents, friends, and your own castoffs are sources for fabrics, hats, and other pieces. Variety stores and grocery stores may have costumes on sale after Halloween. Check costume supply stores (consult the Yellow Pages) and costume catalogues (see *Bibliography*). Try sorting and storing the costume pieces and props in boxes labeled according to category.

Hats are one of the best ways to help an actor assume a character, and hats can be adapted to suit your purposes. Crushable felt hats are good. Flip up the sides, add a feather, and you have a jaunty Jack-in-the-Beanstalk-style hat. Turn the brim down and add twigs or some other off-beat object and create a funny old man's hat. Sew on long ears and create a bunny.

Baseball caps and visors make excellent animal or bird headpieces. Wear the bill forward to create a critter with a snout or bill. Ears may be attached. Turn the bill around for snoutless critters. Pink, orange, or yellow caps or visors are good birds' beaks. Knitted watch caps or fur hats can be used to create animals' heads.

Shawls are theatrical and move well. Shawls with long fringe make beautiful bird wings and are good for characterization because they can be manipulated to show nervousness, flightiness, or grandeur.

Gloves or mittens can almost become puppets. Put them on the hands and wiggle them to create animated berries, flowers, vegetables, twinkling stars, spiders, butterflies, or other insects.

Aprons are good for European folk tale mothers and can be tied around the shoulders to create a cape.

Making No-Sew Costume Pieces

Headband Hats   These can be used to create animals, floral wreaths, and ceremonial headdresses. It is simplest to buy ready-made headbands. For animals, staple or sew on ears. For a floral wreath, twist the stems of plastic flowers around the headband. For a ceremonial headdress, attach feathers, raffia, pipe cleaners, colorful paper, and the like.

Paper Band Hats   Paper band hats can be made of different heights to serve many purposes. To create an animal or headdress, cut a two- to three-inch-wide strip of paper long enough to go around the head with an overlap of an inch. Staple the ends together. Tape or staple paper or real feathers to create a headdress. For animals, add paper ears. To create an African hat, make the band about five inches wide and decorate it with a drawn design.

Paper Band Hat

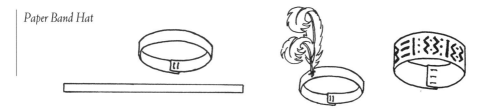

Ceremonial Paper Band Hats With Height   To create a paper band hat with height for a goddess or other ceremonial figure, use tagboard for a sturdy basic band and attach construction paper that is about ten inches high. Decorate with designs, foil, cutouts, fabric, or other media.

Ceremonial Paper Band Hat

Paper Bag Hats   Paper bag hats can be striking and are fun and easy to make. Roll up the opening of a brown shopping bag. Place the bag on the head and crush it into the shape and size desired. Paint the bag or leave it plain and decorate it with feathers, bits of material, or other ornaments. Animal ears or foliage might be added to create specific characters and objects.

Paper Bag Hat

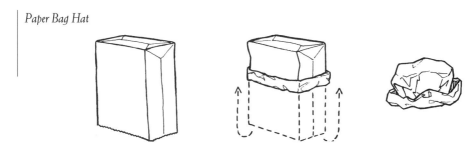

Tunics Tunics can be used for storytellers, characters, and objects such as trees. For a short tunic (for characters needing free movement on stage), buy one yard of forty-five-inch fabric. Fold it in half, and then fold it in half again (quarters). (See diagram.) Make a three-inch cut for the head. To prevent fraying, apply glue around the opening. (Fray Check, available at fabric stores, is good for this purpose.) For a storyteller or long tunic, use two yards of fabric. Tunics can be belted, if desired, using traditional belts or with fabric swatches, scarves, or sashes.

No-Sew Tunics

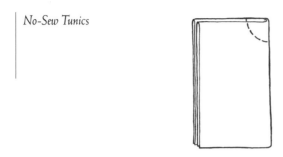

Atmosphere Sticks Streamers of ribbon, fabric, or other materials can be attached to dowels and waved to create atmospheric effects such as pouring rain, dancing flames, or swirling snow. Tape, tie, or tack strips of appropriately colored cloth, ribbons, tinsel, or crepe paper to a dowel. Swirling snow needs strips at least two feet long to create the effect, whereas flames for a fire could be shorter. A hot glue gun can be used to attach tinsel.

Atmosphere Stick

Creating Musical Instruments

It is resourceful and creative for students to make rhythm instruments or discover how to duplicate sounds using ordinary objects. A stimulating way to get students involved and to enrich the play is to give students a few sample ideas and then have them go home and make an instrument on their own. Their inventions are often fascinating. One student strung bottle caps for a rattle. Another made a combination drum-rattle with a gallon bleach bottle containing popcorn kernels.

Encourage students to go into their kitchens and clink, thump, bang, scrape, and strike objects to test their sounds. Nowadays there are so many types of kitchen utensils, gadgets, and containers that the possibilities are endless.

Have students test for sound quality. Some glasses, cups, and pot lids clink and ring nicely; others clunk and thud. In plays performed for an audience, the sound must carry. For example, water in a bottle swished around might create a nice swishing sound, but no one will be able to hear it; a rattle with sand inside is probably not loud enough either.

Students might also try striking or somehow playing different surfaces around the room. A creative teacher found that running a ruler over venetian blinds created a nice storm effect. Encourage students to test things around the classroom or the auditorium where the play will be performed. It is interesting to see how some tables and floors have much better sound quality than others. Exploring sound could be the basis for a spin-off science assignment.

Students might decorate instruments used in performances with ethnic designs. Designs might be drawn and glued in place, or fabrics or wrapping paper with appropriate designs may be used.

Suggestions for quick and easy homemade instruments are given below. (The *Bibliography* in the *Appendix* also suggests books on making instruments and creating sound effects with voice and body.)

- *Rattles*   Any container with a lid or cap may be filled with hard objects such as beans, popcorn, or pebbles.
- *Drums*   A metal wastepaper basket struck with a wooden spoon or the hand; a coffee can; the bottom of a bleach, milk, or juice container.
- *Padded drum stick*   A sock with another sock stuffed inside of it attached to a dowel or ruler.
- *Rhythm sticks*   Two quarter-inch dowels cut one foot long.
- *Gong*   Pot lid struck with a metal spoon.
- *Wood block*   A block of wood, table top, or the wall tapped with a length of dowel or the handle of a wooden spoon. (Pencils and pens make interesting sounds when tapped against the wall, but care must be taken to avoid creating marks on the wall.)
- *Bell*   A glass or ceramic coffee cup that rings when struck by a spoon.
- *Chimes*   Several glasses filled with different levels of water and then struck by a spoon.
- *Triangle*   A glass that gives a *ping* sound when tapped or struck back and forth on the inside with a spoon.

Incorporating Rhythm Instruments

Scripts suggest specific instruments to use to create the sound effects. Many of these instruments are inexpensive. Music education companies often sell complete rhythm band sets. It is best to buy instruments of good quality because they last, are more pleasing to play, and make a better sound.

If possible, furnish some authentic instruments that are traditional in each culture to enhance students' experience. A variety of instruments from different cultures are available at reasonable prices from West Music Company, 1208 5th Street, Coralville, Iowa, 52241. Also check the Yellow Pages for music supply stores.

The following rhythm instruments may be collected to create many effects:

- Tom tom
- Hand drum with sixteen-inch head
- Six-inch triangle
- Jingle bells
- Hand bells
- Tambourine

- Wind chimes
- Guiro (large wooden, fish-shaped scraper with a striker)
- Wood block with a mallet
- Sand blocks
- Shakers, such as maracas or calabash rattles

Using the Piano

The piano is perhaps the most versatile instrument. It can be used to create a great variety of sound effects. If necessary, all of the sound effects required might be accomplished using only the piano by playing the keys in different ways. For example, running fingers along the high notes can create the effect for swirling mist. The whole arm can be held down on the lower keys to create an angry giant's thunderous entrance into a room. A high key played staccato makes an excellent effect for a scurrying mouse or hopping bird. Middle notes played quickly with determination indicate a brisk, no-nonsense stride. One teacher even opened the piano lid and strummed the strings to create the magical harp in *Jack and the Beanstalk*. Two or three students might sit at or stand by the piano and create all of the effects for a play.

CHAPTER THREE

A Model Step-By-Step Rehearsal Schedule

The following gives a step-by-step rehearsal schedule for directing narrative mime plays in a class of thirty-five students or fewer. It uses the Mayan creation myth, *The Creation and the Birth of the Corn God*, as a model.

The approach outlined below has been used in many classrooms. Of course, all the activities are only suggestions, and you will want to use what you need and modify the plan as you see fit. Chapter One describes some of these techniques in more detail, and some methods and activities presented in Chapter One are repeated here to give a detailed rehearsal schedule.

Getting Started

Each play in this book runs about twenty-five minutes. On-stage rehearsals should last at least one hour. More than one step of the rehearsal process might be presented in a session, and some steps, such as blocking the play, might take more than one session to complete.

The ongoing study of the culture at hand can extend over several weeks and can be presented before, during, and after the performance of the cultural myth or tale. It is best, however, to produce the play itself in two weeks or less. A short time frame focuses students' enthusiasm, involvement, and commitment.

Introducing the Culture

Goal To give students background on the particular culture in order to deepen their appreciation for the myth they will perform.

Materials Books on the culture and its stories. (See *Bibliography*.) Story questions and research topics follow the script.

Procedure Tell students they will study the great ancient Mayan culture and perform a play based on a Mayan myth called *The Creation and the Birth of the Corn God*.

Study topics might include the role and importance of corn; how the character and temperament of the people contributed to their success; achievements in art, architecture, and astronomy; and the concept of time. Students might also study Mayan lifestyle in the past and present, including clothes, musical instruments, diet, pottery, jewelry, hairstyles, homes, and temples.

Introducing the Play

Goal To introduce the play and discuss the characters so that students can begin thinking about how they might play them.

Materials A copy of the script for each class member. The script, as defined by the decorative border, can be photocopied from this book.

Procedure Mention the different roles students might play in the production. Students read the script together as a class and discuss the characters.

Informal Classroom Dramatization

Goal To teach students how to act informally in the classroom as preparation for a stage performance.

Materials One copy of the Mayan creation myth script for each of the four class groups. The script, as defined by the decorative border, can be photocopied from this book.

Procedure Using the classroom dramatization methods described in the script and Chapter Four, *Informal Classroom Dramatizations*, students act the myth and then evaluate each other's dramatization. If desired, students might also learn acting techniques using *Dramatizing Aesop's Fables*, published by Dale Seymour Publications, which provides scripts written specifically for classroom dramatization. (See *Bibliography*.)

Explaining How the Play Will Be Produced

Goal To give students an overview of how the play will be performed.

Materials Stage-layout diagram, as given in Chapter One.

Procedure Draw the stage-layout diagram on the chalkboard and describe it. Point out the seating arrangement of the actors, storytellers, and sound crew. Mention that everyone wears all black clothing to create an ensemble or team feeling and to help show off the costume pieces and props.

Describe how actors playing both characters and inanimate objects keep their props and costume pieces under their chairs and pick them up, put them on, or use them according to cues in the script.

Point out how the sound crew's table and a piano are at an angle so that the crew can see the stage action and can be seen by the audience as they make their effects.

Introducing and Learning the Stage Areas

Goal To teach students the basic stage areas so that they can move to them as directed.

Materials Stage-area diagram, as given in Chapter One.

Procedure Explain that different areas on the stage have names to help the director indicate to the actors where they should be positioned at a given time. Draw the stage-area diagram on the chalkboard.

Explain that the term *upstage* comes from a time when stages sloped upward so that audiences seated at one level could see what was happening at the back of the stage. *Downstage* is the opposite of upstage. *Stage right* and *stage left* are identified from the actors' point of view, and *center* is obviously the center of the stage. Have students practice moving to the different areas as you direct. Suggest that students who have trouble differentiating right from left put a sticker on their shoe or sleeve as a reminder.

Presenting the Written Tryout

Goal To let students express in writing what role they want to play and to get them actively involved in thinking about the characters and how they might portray them.

Procedure Have students reread the play silently. Explain that the written tryout does not guarantee that everyone will get the part he or she wants.

On the chalkboard or on a chart, list the following points for students to include in the written tryout:

- List three roles you want to play in order of preference, including characters, inanimate objects, storytellers, or sound crew.
- Describe the characteristics of the character or what is required to perform the role.
- Explain why you should be chosen to play the role.

Training Actors and Holding an Informal Acting Tryout

Goal To train actors by practicing the three acting principles while enacting characters and scenes from the play. Take this opportunity to observe who might be best to play major roles as a sort of informal acting tryout. It is most beneficial if some of these or other acting activities (made up by the students or teacher) are done before every rehearsal as warm-up exercises.

Materials List *Belief, Control,* and *Voice and Movement* on the chalkboard; use the acting exercises that accompany the script; use a bell to indicate the beginning and end of each exercise.

Procedure Explain that good actors follow three acting principles. Discuss each principle separately and then apply it to the acting exercises.

- Belief

Discuss why it is necessary for a good actor to believe or really pretend to be the character being portrayed in order to make it seem real. Play the Moon Goddess by walking casually and acting like yourself. Ask how an audience would feel about your portrayal. Have students do the *Becoming the Moon Goddess or Sun God* activity and the *Molding and Becoming Mud People* and *Carving and Becoming Wood People* activities from Chapter Six to practice belief. Students evaluate each other's believable acting, describing specifically how voice and movement were used to make the acting believable.

- Control

Ask what it means for actors to use control over their movements and voices to make the performance artistic and focused. Model what it looks like when a dancer or baseball pitcher's movements are out of control.

Have students do the *Becoming Destructive, Angry Rain* activity in Chapter Six to practice control. First discuss movements that the group might do to portray destructive, angry rain in a controlled, artistic way.

- Voice and Movement

Ask what it means for an actor to use voice and movement to show a character's personality and feelings. Demonstrate by saying the word *voice* twice, first in the powerful Sun God's voice and then in a tiny mouse's voice. Next say *movement* twice, first taking the regal, commanding stance of the Sun God and then taking the stance of a timorous mouse.

Have students do the *Character Transformation With Sound Effects* activity in Chapter Six to practice using voice and movement to become the objects and animals in the myth.

Vocal Stage Training

Goal To teach and practice the vocal techniques needed in order to communicate a play effectively and dramatically to an audience.

Materials List *Projection, Diction,* and *Colorization* on a chart or on the chalkboard.

Procedure Explain that there are three vocal techniques performers need to use when putting on a play for an audience. Mention that actors take voice classes to learn and practice these techniques.

Discuss each principle separately and then practice it, using speeches and dialogue from the play. Students should stand for all vocal exercises.

- Projection

Ask students to define projection. Model by projecting your voice as you say the word *projection*. Have students say it with you.

Ask what happens to the audience if an actor does not project. Use projection as you perform the following introduction from the script. Pause after each line to let students repeat it with you. Encourage them to project their voices.

The Creation

A Mayan myth of how the world began.

First there was only heaven...

...and the Sea.

Only the Sun God and the Moon Goddess stood majestically
in the rippling water.

The Moon Goddess called for Earth.

- Diction

Discuss diction or pronouncing every sound or syllable in a word clearly, particularly the final consonants. Demonstrate by saying *earth*, emphatically pronouncing the /th/. Then say *earth* with poor diction, swallowing the final /th/. Ask why it is important for actors, storytellers, and all public speakers to have good diction.

Practice saying words from the script that end in consonants, such as *creation*, *mists, river, bird, wood*. Have students repeat each word after you. Then try the following play narration using both good projection and diction.

Gracias students, adults, too,

For watching so kindly our show for you.

Of a Mayan myth, old yet new.

We hope it came alive for you.

And here's a last tip from us, your friends.

Read a book of these myths from beginning to end.

And study different cultures wherever they may be.

For the more that you know,

The more you'll be free.

- Colorization

Ask what it means for actors and other speakers to put color in their voices to make their speech come alive. Say *colorization*, making your voice sound colorful. Have students say it.

Practice saying descriptive words, making your voice sound like what each word describes. Descriptive words that are opposites are good for this activity. For example, say the word *hot* and make your voice sound boiling hot. Say *cold* and make it sound freezing cold. Try *big* and *little, high* and *low, joyful* and *depressed, mighty* and *timid, angry* and *calm, funny* and *sad, nervous* and *serene, mean* and *kind*. You might also wish to try names of colors.

The Formal Tryout—Flexible Casting

Goal   To let students try out for two or three parts they want to play; to determine who is able to use projection, diction, and colorization to communicate a character to an audience.

Materials   A copy of the script for each class member.

Procedure   Explain that students will now try out for the parts they want and remind them that an essential requirement for storytellers and major characters is good projection so that the audience can hear and understand the play. Explain that those playing a character should concentrate on voice and movement.

Explain that all casting is flexible and that if someone is absent or does not work out for some reason, the part will be reassigned. Mention that unfortunately not everyone will get the part they most want, and that even the best professional actors do not get every role they want.

Have students try out for two or three roles by reading and acting from portions of the script. You may wish to give yourself until the next day to make your decisions and announce the cast. Students not wanting to try out for principle parts will be on the sound crew or will play inanimate objects. Use the written tryouts to help you assign these roles.

Highlighting Storyteller and Sound Crew Parts

Goal To prepare students to rehearse so that the storytellers and sound crew will be ready to perform on cue.

Materials Copies of the script and highlighting pens for storytellers and sound crew members only.

Procedure Explain that only the storytellers and sound crew use scripts at rehearsals, and it is essential that they highlight their parts so that they will come in, or perform, on cue. Otherwise the flow of the narration will be disrupted.

Explain that actors do not use scripts on stage so that they are able to move freely. Actors' lines are virtually fed to them by storytellers, and if they forget a line, a storyteller will give it to them or they can make up what to say.

On-Stage Rehearsals

Arrange for all of the actual rehearsing of the play to be done on the stage or in the area where the play will be performed so that students become comfortable with it.

Learning The Opening Dance

Goal To teach the opening dance.

Materials Dance instructions and taped music suggestions as given in the *Production Notes* for the script.

Procedure Explain that the play begins and ends with a traditional dance of the culture and that a sound crew member will play the music for the dance on the tape recorder. Mention that performers may dance, sit and sway or move to the music, or perhaps shake rattles or bells to blend with the music. Practice the steps and stances for the dance.

Introducing Blocking Techniques

Goal To teach students the movement techniques that will enable them to share the play effectively and dramatically with an audience.

Procedure Explain that you will give actors blocking or movement instructions during rehearsals so that they will know where to go when. Mention the two blocking techniques that actors need to know to ensure that the audience can see what is happening on the stage and enjoy the show:

• Open up to the audience.
• Don't get blocked.

Demonstrate both techniques, using the guidelines provided in Chapter One.

Blocking the Plays

Goal   To give students their stage movements.

Materials   Basic introductory costume and prop materials; in this case, blue fabric for the Sea, white Mist atmosphere sticks, dark brown cloth for Mud People, tan cloth for Wood People (see *Costume Suggestions* for each script).

Procedure   Blocking takes about two hours for each play. Chapter One describes in detail techniques of effective blocking. The stage set-up illustrated for each script suggests where to place inanimate objects and scenery actors.

With this type of production, blocking can be loose and flexible. The only essentials are that actors be visible to everyone in the audience and do not cover each other, that the focus is on the main action occurring on the stage at a given time, and that the whole stage is used in scenes with lots of movement so that the action does not look cramped.

Begin introducing costume pieces and props from the first rehearsal so that students get used to using them. They are an integral part of the production and also stimulate interest and imagination. Use only a few at the first rehearsal (see suggested materials above) and add a few more to each subsequent rehearsal.

Developing Acting, Speaking, and Sound Effect Skills

Goal   To develop acting, narrating, and sound effect techniques to communicate the play theatrically to the audience.

Procedure   Chapter One describes how to train each member of the performance team to communicate their parts effectively and dramatically. These skills should be emphasized and practiced during every rehearsal. As mentioned, it is good to begin each rehearsal with some acting exercises to get students involved and warmed up.

Polishing the Play—Three Dress Rehearsals

It is good to have three dress rehearsals—two back-to-back dress rehearsals the day before the performance and a final warm-up dress rehearsal just before the performance.

The first dress rehearsal is a stop-and-start dress rehearsal to polish rough spots. The second is a non-stop run-through to help the performers get a feel for how the action will flow for a performance.

With beginners, it is highly desirable to rehearse immediately before the first performance to warm up, get students involved in the acting, and help work out nervous jitters.

The central emphasis at all of these rehearsals is to build confidence, particularly by reinforcing what students do well. The following suggests how to conduct these rehearsals.

First Dress Rehearsal

Goal To polish major rough spots and to build confidence.

Materials All costumes and props (see *Costume Suggestions* for the script).

Procedure Explain that there will be two dress rehearsals, one after the other. The first is to polish rough spots, stopping along the way to work out problems. The second will be a straight run-through.

During the first polishing rehearsal, correct major flaws such as speaking too softly or not performing enthusiastically enough, but also give plenty of verbal encouragement. At the end of this rehearsal, discuss what was good about the rehearsal and what might be improved next time.

Second Dress Rehearsal

Goal To build students' confidence and enthusiasm and to teach them how to work as a team and perform even if something goes wrong.

Procedure During this rehearsal, try to bring in a few sympathetic observers to give the performers the experience and excitement of an audience.

Explain again that this is a non-stop rehearsal, and no matter what happens, students must cover it up and go on. Discuss with students what they might do if an actor forgets a line, drops a prop, or has difficulty with a costume piece. Mention that even in professional theatre there are mistakes. Ask why the audience usually does not notice when something goes wrong.

After this rehearsal, heartily praise what was done well. Students need this reassurance to be excited and confident for the performance the following day.

Warm-Up Rehearsal

Goal To warm students up, to focus their nervous jitters into effective performing, and to build confidence for a successful performance.

Procedure Explain that students will have the chance to warm up by running through the play once more before the audience arrives. Mention all the things that performers have been doing well in order to boost confidence. Ask them what they might do to create a good performance. Students' comments at this time are often most perceptive and helpful.

During this rehearsal, take note of who acts nervous or makes a lot of errors so that you can be ready to help with a few encouraging words in the performance counseling session just prior to the performance.

The Performance

Following the warm-up dress rehearsal, it is wise to prepare both the students and the audience for the performance. After the performance, follow-up activities will enhance the experience for all involved.

Before Performance Counseling

Goal To build confidence and give students guidance and reassurance to help them enjoy the experience and do their best.

Procedure Nervousness before a performance is normal even for professionals. Performing before an audience is exhilarating and a little nerve-wracking. Performers need the director's guidance and reassurance to gain a feeling of confidence. Ways to avoid the burden of perfectionism are suggested in Chapter One.

Psychologist Jack Sanford suggests asking how each student is feeling just before the performance. This acknowledges the students' feelings and shows that you as a director care. If some say they are nervous, reassure them by explaining that jitters are normal and that all performers feel them.

Then reassure all students individually that they are doing a great job. It is helpful to point out one specific thing that each student does well. This helps students focus on what they do well and may help them improve it even further in the performance.

To help the sound crew be ready and secure, check that they all have their first instruments ready in front of them so that they can perform on cue.

Training the Audience and Acknowledging Their Role

Goal To train the audience to observe what performers do to create a good performance; to acknowledge the audience's significant role; to give the performers final performance tips.

Procedure This play and production style offers many opportunities for the audience to get involved. It also develops the imagination and lets the audience experience directly how theatre works, since many of the theatrics are out in the open for all to see.

Counsel the audience before the performance. Explain that the play is a myth of the great Mayan culture, called *The Creation and The Birth of the Corn God*. Ask the audience to observe how the actors use their voices and bodies to pretend and make believe that they are the characters they are playing. Give examples such as watching to see how the Moon Goddess uses her voice and body to give a majestic portrayal. Mention several other characters—such as the swooping Orange Bird, the jagged Rain, the swirling Mist—and explain how these actors will use their voices and bodies to play their parts. This also gives the actors some last-minute reminders.

Tell the audience to watch the storytellers and see what they do with their voices and bodies to make the story exciting; point out the sound crew and have the audience watch how it makes sound effects to go with the action to help the actors act their parts.

Explain that after the performance you will ask the audience to tell you and the performers what they liked about the production.

Audience Follow-Up Discussion

Goal   To reiterate the importance of the audience and to give the audience a chance to voice its reactions to the performance; to give the performers positive feedback; to train the audience by elaborating on their comments, pointing out the skills necessary to achieve what they liked.

Procedure   Thank the audience for being attentive, expressing your and the performers' appreciation. Ask audience members to stand up one at a time and say loudly what they enjoyed so that everyone can hear what they have to say. Respond to their reactions, pointing out the skills required to carry out what they liked. For example, if someone likes the Mud People, point out how they really stood like people of mud and sagged and fell as if they were full of water. If someone mentions the dance movements, reinforce how the performers focused on moving gracefully to the music. Make sure that every performance element is included—characters, objects, storytellers, and sound crew. Elicit comments on performances that are not mentioned.

Audience Follow-Up—Writing, Art, and Reading

Goal   To give the audience a chance to reflect on the performance through art and writing; to use this performance to stimulate viewers to read more tales, and perhaps to dramatize them; to give the performers written and artistic feedback.

Procedure   Tell the audience that you and the performers would greatly appreciate letters and pictures describing favorite parts of the performance. Mention that these will be read and displayed in the classroom and kept in a special book.

Performers' Follow-Up and Reflection

Goal   To give the performers an opportunity to describe their reaction to the experience and reflect on its meaning to them.

Procedure   Performing is a heightened, meaningful experience. A follow-up reflection session helps students articulate what the experience meant to them and artistically evaluate the performance. Reflection also provides a calm transition back to the daily business of the classroom and is an ideal opportunity to take advantage of students' excitement and enthusiasm to discuss possible future drama projects, including other assembly plays or informal classroom dramatizations. There are always students who are highly excited by the experience and who want to do more.

Some possible reflection questions include the following:

- What did you enjoy most during this production?
- What was most difficult?
- What was your reaction to having an audience?
- How did you feel during the performance?

Students might make their own classroom album describing and drawing their favorite part of the performance.

CHAPTER FOUR

Informal Classroom Dramatizations

The narrative mime plays in this book can readily be adapted for informal classroom presentations and are stimulating and easy to do for beginners. Performing in the classroom gives students a chance to develop their imaginations and learn acting skills in a relaxed atmosphere. It also gives everyone a chance to experiment with playing a number of parts.

There are two ways in which narrative mime scripts can be used in the classroom: *Circle Story Dramatization* and *Segmented Story Dramatization*. In Circle Story Dramatization, students cast in various roles sit in a circle, stepping into the center to act their parts as the storytellers cue them. Begin by reading the storytellers' narration yourself. Then have students take these roles. This is a very organized way to dramatize a story and might be used before trying the Segmented Story Dramatization.

For the Segmented Story Dramatization, the play is divided into scenes. Students in groups practice their scenes on their own and then present them to the class.

The following describes how to use these two approaches with the scripts in this book. As with preparing a dramatization for an audience, it is always best to discuss the principles of good acting (see Chapter One) and do the acting exercises given with each script.

Circle Story Dramatization

Students benefit from Circle Story Dramatization because they learn acting principles and techniques to create an instant performance. The circle formation bonds the group, gets everyone involved, and introduces students to theater-in-the-round.

Present some of the acting activities given with the script as a warm-up and then assign roles, doubling up parts as necessary. Arrange students in a circle in the order they will appear. Then say "Curtain," ding a triangle, or ring a bell to signal that the play has begun. Narrate the story, having students step into the circle to act their roles and return to their seats when done.

When the reading is finished, have all the players bow and then sit down. Students evaluate the acting, discussing who played their parts believably, what they did to make them believable, and what might be added next time to improve the performance. Repeat the dramatization, casting students as storytellers and reassigning roles.

Use the following techniques to adapt scripts for Circle Story Dramatization:

- Use only a few props or costumes, or eliminate them entirely.
- Eliminate the sound effects. Students might vocalize effects or create effects using their bodies or objects available in the room.
- Eliminate the need for characters to say the exact dialogue in the script. Students might create their own dialogue, or they may simply mime the action. If pertinent dialogue is needed that does not spring from a cue given by the storyteller, the storyteller might say the line and have the character repeat it.
- Use only one storyteller to read all of the storytellers' parts.

Segmented Story Dramatization

Segmented Story Dramatization promotes teamwork and allows students to develop their own ideas as they independently create the play scenes. It teaches students play structure; plays are often divided into scenes and rehearsed that way. Students working in groups are able to observe and be inspired by each other's innovative creativity, and they can look at a performance objectively to evaluate what was effective artistically and what might be improved.

Scripts adapted for this method are divided into scenes; each scene has a cast list showing the number of students needed to act it. Make one copy of the play for each storyteller and assign students to appropriate groups.

Send groups to various areas in the room to practice their scenes. Have students decide who will play the storyteller, characters, and sound crew if they decide to use effects, and have them practice dramatizing the story. They might also do the acting exercises after they practice their scenes in order to deepen characterization and involvement.

The groups should have about fifteen minutes to practice. Keep the time brief to focus commitment and creativity. Students then reassemble and present their scenes in order of appearance in the story.

Tell students that their goals are to move smoothly from one scene to another and to create the feeling of a whole play with no big breaks between the action. You will help them by following the guidelines below:

- Call the scene number and slowly count to five as the actors take their positions and get ready to act the scene. (A limited period of time helps students take their places quickly.)
- Say "Curtain" immediately after counting to five. This signals to students that the action is about to begin.
- Say "Freeze." Actors freeze in an opening picture at the beginning of the scene.
- Storytellers narrate the scene as the actors perform it.
- Say "Freeze" again at the end of the scene. Actors make a frozen picture of the final moment of their scene.
- Call the next scene number and slowly count to five again as the actors take their places so that the play can continue.

After all students have done their presentations, students evaluate each other's performances, discussing who played their parts believably, what they did to make them believable, and what might be added next time to improve the acting.

Have the same or different groups practice and perform their scenes again, using the suggestions given by peers and the teacher and their own new ideas. The groups might also perform the play in the classroom for parents or other classes, adding a few costume pieces and props.

Following are specific guidelines and ideas for informally dramatizing each of the plays in this book.

Dramatizing *Talk, Talk, Talk* Informally

Talk, Talk, Talk may be dramatized informally in the classroom using Circle Story Dramatization or Segmented Story Dramatization. The following specific suggestions may also be used.

- To help students playing inanimate objects remember the tag dialogue that they repeat several times, write their lines on sentence strips or index cards. When their dialogue comes up, they stand and read it from the cards. They might also, of course, memorize it.
- Have the same students play the inanimate objects throughout the Segmented Story Dramatization to keep continuity and to prevent groups from getting too big. Students playing inanimate objects simply sit in their chairs and pop up to say their dialogue. When working in groups for the Segmented Story Dramatization, the storyteller might read the inanimate object's tag dialogue if the student playing that object is in another scene.
- In both methods, the whole class participates in the chorus, as outlined in the play. Students might also be chosen to make the sound effects to accompany the inanimate objects, according to the script. The class should practice the acting activities ahead of time so they know what to do.

Dramatizing *The Creation and the Birth of the Corn God* Informally

The Mayan myth may be dramatized informally in the classroom using Circle Story Dramatization or Segmented Story Dramatization.

Dramatizing *Coyote and the Swallowing Monster* Informally

The following specific ideas may be implemented when using both the Circle Story Dramatization and Segmented Story Dramatization techniques with the Native American myth:

- Have the storyteller say any pertinent character dialogue and the character repeat it if the dialogue does not spring naturally from the cues in the script.
- Have the whole class respond as the Monster and all of the other group parts. Students should first practice the *Becoming the Monster Chorus* activity in the acting exercises provided.

Dramatizing *The Crane Maiden* Informally

Use either Circle Story Dramatization or Segmented Story Dramatization to dramatize this play informally.

Dramatizing *Jack and the Beanstalk* Informally

To help students fully experience the characters and their situations, have them use their own dialogue and creative ideas to dramatize the scenes suggested below. Explain that scenes in plays have a conflict—one person wants something that another is reluctant to give, and finally there is a resolution. Usually in a conflict one character does not give in too easily but needs to be convinced. Often both have to give in a little to create a resolution; there must be give and take, and it must be dramatically interesting and lively.

Divide the class into pairs or groups to act out the twelve scenes. Have students create scenes using the beginning, middle, and end provided to resolve the conflict so that there is some give and take. After fifteen minutes of rehearsal, students present their scenes in order.

Scene One Jack's mother is worried. Jack has to convince her he can sell the cow. Cow shows through mime that she does not want to be sold.

Scene Two Jack meets the old man. The old man examines the cow. The old man has to convince Jack to sell the cow for beans. Cow shows through pantomime that she wants to go off with the old man.

Scene Three Jack returns and Mother wants to know how much he got for the cow. Jack tries to convince her that the beans are magic. Mother throws the beans out the window and sends Jack to bed with no supper.

Scene Four Jack wakes up. He sees the marvelous beanstalk and climbs up. He goes to Giant's house. He has to convince Giant's Wife to give him breakfast. Giant's Wife does. Jack eats, but they hear Giant and Jack hides in the oven.

Scene Five Giant enters and smells all around. "Fe, Fi, Fo, Fum." Giant's Wife has to convince Giant no one is there. Giant's Wife tells Giant to wash up. Giant's Wife gives Giant breakfast. He eats greedily. Giant gets the gold, counts it, falls asleep, and snores.

Scene Six Jack sneaks out of the oven. He steals the gold. He climbs down the beanstalk. Mother is overjoyed with the gold. They discuss how they will spend it.

Scene Seven Jack climbs up the beanstalk again. He wants breakfast again. Giant's Wife is suspicious. Jack has to convince her to let him in. Jack gets breakfast. They hear Giant. Jack hides in the oven.

Scene Eight Giant arrives again. He smells Jack. "Fe, Fi, Fo, Fum." Giant is famished and eats breakfast. He calls for Hen and tells it to lay. Hen cackles and lays golden eggs—small, bigger, biggest. Giant falls asleep and snores.

Scene Nine Jack sneaks out of the oven without waking Giant. He grabs Hen. Hen cackles. Jack goes down the beanstalk. He shows Mother the Hen and how it lays golden eggs. Mother is thrilled.

Scene Ten Jack climbs the beanstalk for the third time. He hides behind bushes.

Giant's Wife gets a pail of water. Jack hides in the broom closet. Giant's Wife thinks someone is there but cannot find anyone. This scene may be done all in mime, or the characters might talk to themselves.

Scene Eleven   Giant comes home for the third time. Giant smells Jack. "Fe, Fi, Fo, Fum." Giant and Giant's Wife look all around. Giant eats breakfast. Giant calls for Harp. Harp sings. Giant sleeps.

Scene Twelve   Jack sneaks from closet and grabs Harp. Harp calls to Giant. Jack runs to the beanstalk. Giant is running behind, running in slow motion through the clouds. Jack climbs down the beanstalk and chops it down. Giant breaks through the earth. Jack and Mother live happily ever after with Hen and Harp.

PART TWO

Developing Scripts for Myths and Tales

CHAPTER FIVE

Talk, Talk, Talk
A West African Folk Tale

Variations of this folk tale are well known in different parts of Africa. The story involves a number of objects and animals who astound people by talking to them. In this version from Ghana, the talking animals and objects shock a community by speaking to a farmer, fisherman, weaver, and eventually to the chief of the land.

One day, while digging in the garden, a farmer hears the angry complaints of some yams. After a dog, two trees, and some rocks also speak, the frightened farmer runs away. The farmer relays the incident to a fisherman, who reacts with scorn and disbelief until a fishing net also speaks. The two run in panic until they reach a weaver, who also does not believe the story until some woven cloth speaks. The three approach the chief to tell their stories. The angry chief reacts with disdain until the ceremonial stools speak as well, leaving the entire community in an amusing uproar.

Acting Exercises

The following acting exercises may be used to help students practice acting principles and develop the characters that make up the cast of this play.

Practicing Mimed Chants

Goal To practice the African theatre technique of miming repetitive actions and saying repeated words and phrases vigorously, so that every word looks and sounds like what it means.

Acting Principle Voice and Movement.

Optional Materials List the following action words on a chart or on the chalkboard and point to them as students respond.

Procedure Lead the following mimed chants to model vigorous group participation. Later you may wish to have a student lead the group.

- "Dig." (Say it and mime movement six times.)
- "DIG!" (Say once explosively.)
- "Ripple." (Say four times and imitate a river.)
- Stomp (Show anger, determination; four times.)
- Stride (Show casual, in-charge attitude; four times.)
- Skip (Show carefree attitude; four times.)
- "Ha!" (Laugh scornfully; four times)

Character Transformation

Goal To experience each character's basic stance and actions.

Acting Principle Belief.

Materials A bell. You may wish to write each character's name and tag dialogue on cards or on a chart.

Procedure Explain that students will use characters' actions and dialogue in quick transformations. Work on one character at a time. Ring the bell to start the action. Have students perform the characters' actions, as given below, and then freeze after the action in order to say the dialogue. The class might be divided in half with each half acting every other one of the actions. All actions are done in place.

- Farmer: Pick up a heavy shovel, push it deep into the earth to dig yams, toss a heavy shovelful of dirt over your shoulder. Hear something underground. Freeze. Look for the source of the sound.
- Yam hidden deep underground: Feel a shovel bite into your skin. Freeze. "Ouch." Feel the shovel bite into you deeper. Freeze. "Stop! Stop!"
- Dog: Bounce over to the farmer to tell him the truth. Freeze. "It was the yams. The yams said, 'Stop digging me up!'"
- Rock: Growl at the farmer for dropping branches on you. Freeze. "Don't put that branch on me."
- Fisherman: Stride confidently. Freeze. Laugh scornfully at farmer, "Ha, ha, ha, ha."

- Net: Wiggle enthusiastically. Freeze. "Did he put that branch down?"
- Weaver: Happy-go-lucky, skipping. Freeze. Laugh at farmer and fisherman, "Ha, ha, ha, ha."
- Kente cloth: Display your beauty. Freeze. Pop up perkily. "I don't think he's crazy."
- Servant: March officially. Freeze. "There is an emergency."
- Stool bearer: Scurry to get the stool in place. Freeze. Bow humbly several times.
- Umbrella bearer: Run in place to cover every inch of the Chief. Freeze.
- Golden ceremonial stool: Display your ornaments proudly. Freeze. "Whoever heard of a talking yam?"
- Chief: Pompous know-it-all; parade domineeringly. Freeze. "What nonsense."

Character Pop Up

Goal   To coordinate acting with sound effects.

Acting Principles   Belief, Voice and Movement, Control.

Materials   Wood block, bass drum, a variety of rattles, tambourine, jingle bells.

Procedure   Farmer, Fisherman, and Weaver stand center stage. The objects sit in their chairs. Farmer, Fisherman, and Weaver give the following cues. The objects then stand, take character stance, say lines excitedly, freeze, wait for sound effect, and sit. The sound crew plays the effect that follows the line of dialogue. Effect must be done briskly and with dramatic excitement.

FARMER: "I was digging yams, and they said..."

YAMS (*holding up hands*): Stop, Stop.

SOUND CREW: Wood block.

FARMER: My dog said...

DOG (*holding up paws*): Stop digging those yams.

SOUND CREW: Bass drum.

FARMER: The palm trees said...

TREES (*shaking fingers*): Don't hit that dog.

SOUND CREW: Rattles.

FARMER: And the rocks said...

ROCK (*raising fists*): Grrr. Don't put that branch on me.

SOUND CREW: Tambourine.

FISHERMAN: My net wiggled...

NET (*wiggling*): Did he put the branch down?

SOUND CREW: Jingle bells.

WEAVER: The cloths said...

CLOTHS (*popping up heads*): I don't think he's crazy.

SOUND CREW: Wood block.

Chanting Like a Drum Beat

Goal To involve everyone in the Run Chant, repeated five times during the play. Actors pump arms vigorously, as if running a distance. Chant resembles a drumbeat.

Acting Principle Voice and Movement.

Materials Wood block or bass drum.

Procedure Storyteller One, who leads all the Run Chants, gives the cue used every time. Students might sit and pump their arms in a low position the first time the chant is done and raise their arms as if running faster for each subsequent chant. This will make the chant build in dramatic excitement. Younger students may prefer to sit and run. The accent is on the first *run* in each sequence and ends with a final, explosive *run!* with hands thrust out forward and frozen. Begin by using a drum beat to accompany the chant, to give students a sense of how the chant should sound. Once students understand the concept, the drum will no longer be necessary.

STORYTELLER ONE (*turning to performers*): ...and they began to...

CHORUS (*pumping arms as if running*): *Run,* run, run, run. *Run,* run, run, run. *Run,* run, run, run. (*explosively*) *Run!*

Express and Freeze

Goal To loosen inhibitions; to promote creative fluidity; to train students in the African theatre style of total body expression.

Acting Principles Belief, Voice and Movement, Control.

Procedure Explain that African theatre is physical and expressive, using the entire face and body to express feelings and emotions. In rapid succession, students should show the following emotions with their whole body and then freeze: Joy, Surprise, Fear, Hate, Anguish, Depression, Revenge, Deep concern, Struggle, Triumph. Encourage students to experiment with different body movements and positions to express each of the emotions. Students might also brainstorm other emotions to show.

Production Notes

The following guidelines may be used to enhance the quality of the production with dance movements and simple costumes.

African Yam Dance

Music "Chohun and Gyamadud," a Ghana street dance from the audio tape entitled *Ancient Ceremonies, Dance Music and Songs of Ghana,* recorded in Ghana by Stephen Jay. Electra/Asylum/Nonesuch Records, 75 Rockefeller Plaza, New York, NY, 10019. (Any appropriate African music or drumming accompaniment may be substituted.)

Purpose and Style To celebrate as a community the new crop of yams. The energetic, vital, total-body involvement has an improvisational quality but strictly follows the beat of the drum.

Materials Students may wear colorful scarves or strips of African-style fabric tied around their heads. Sound crew may accompany the taped music with drum beats and rattles.

Formation   A line facing the audience; movement is forward and back.

Steps and Stances   Feet are flat on the ground; body is often close to the ground, symbolizing a close contact with Mother Earth; flexible, rotating shoulder movements. There are four steps—the Sit Down, the Knee Up, the Rooster, and the Pull.

Step One: At the opening of the play, dancers sit in their chairs, waiting for the music to begin. When the music begins, the leader stands and does the Sit Down step to upstage center. The dancer stoops or "sits down" with feet apart and hands by sides, elbows raised slightly to resemble wings. In this position, the dancer walks forward, rhythmically moving the body side to side.

Sit Down Step

Step Two: Arriving upstage center, the leader freezes. The other dancers stand and do the Sit Down step, joining the leader in a line. All do the Sit Down step toward the audience. The line need not be perfectly straight, and no one has to be doing the movement at the exact same time as anyone else, but everyone should follow the drum beat.

Step Three: Immediately upon reaching the front, the leader moves backward upstage, facing the audience and doing the Knee Up step. The dancer puts arms behind the back and locks hands together. One knee is raised up to the chest as high as possible. That leg is lowered and then the other knee is raised up as high as possible. Movement continues in this fashion. Dancers follow leader.

Knee Up Step

Step Four: Reaching upstage, the leader does the Rooster step, moving downstage. This step is like the Sit Down except that the hands are on the hips to resemble wings. The pronounced side-to-side movement resembles the movement of a parading rooster. All dancers follow leader.

Rooster Step

Step Five: Arriving downstage, the leader does the Pull step, moving upstage. The dancer thrusts arms forward, slightly toward the right, and pretends to pull them through water, almost like a paddling motion to one side. Repeat the movement, thrusting the arms toward the left, stepping back each time. Again, all dancers follow the leader.

Pull Step

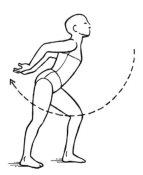

Dancers do the Rooster step to their seats. Music fades completely as the last dancer sits. The actors put on their costume pieces, and Storyteller One begins the first lines of the play, speaking in an enthusiastic voice to grab the audience's attention.

Finale: African dance is spontaneous, improvisational, and rhythmic. For the final dance after the play, encourage students to use the steps from the opening dance or make up their own movements. Perhaps invite members of the audience to dance too.

Costume Suggestions

For narrative mime presentations, all students wear black clothing—black shirts and black pants—with individual character costumes worn as additional pieces to the all-black attire.

Storytellers   African-style batik or other fabric can be made into tunics (see Chapter Two, *Setting the Scene*, for no-sew tunics), or study pictures of African fashions and tie and drape the fabric over the shoulder appropriately. Use a variety of colorful fabrics. Girls might wrap colorful scarves around their heads.

Farmer   Short tunic of orange African-style material and farmer-style straw hat with same fabric used for a headband.

Yams   Dark purple mittens.

Cow   Black fur hat with horns attached.

Dog   Black-and-white dog ears attached to a headband.

Palm Tree   Green tunic with pointed, stylized palm frond edges.

Rock   No costume other than black clothing is necessary. Actors use their bodies to form the shape of a rock.

Fisherman   Tunic of blue African-style fabric.

Rippling River   Bright blue, light fabric.

Net   Big crocheted shawl, light fish net, or nylon net big enough to cover the Net actors.

Weaver   African-style tunic and head wrap in shades of red to differentiate from Fisherman and Farmer.

Kente Cloth   Three lengths of cloth with different patterns, resembling kente cloth if possible. Colors should be bright orange, maroon, green, blue, and some black. Study pictures or examples of African fabric.

Servant   Gray or other neutral color of African-style fabric tied on the shoulder.

Dresser   Tunic cut in front to create a jacket, and a colorful head scarf if the part is played by a girl.

Stool Bearer   Tunic cut in front to create a jacket, and a colorful turban if the part is played by a girl.

Umbrella Bearer   Tunic cut in front to create a jacket. Fabric should be different from that of the Dresser. Head scarf can also be different.

Umbrella   Umbrella of a bright color or pattern. Perhaps tie or glue on strips of fabric or yarn to give it a ceremonial feeling.

Chief   Tunic of gold and black tiger print, large gold pendant, decorative headdress (see *Selected Bibliography* for books with images illustrating headdress styles).

Golden Ceremonial Stool   Played by three students lined up in a row. The two on the end might hold up dowels with gold tinsel or strips of gold fabric tied on them for a ceremonial look.

Talk, Talk, Talk

A West African Folk Tale

Cast

STORYTELLER 1 (leader; very responsible; strong voice)

STORYTELLERS 2, 3, 4 (strong voices; ability to follow and pick up cues)

FARMER (leading role; energetic; enthusiastic; strong voice)

YAM (2)

COW (deep voice; heavy, relaxed movement)

DOG (bouncy, enthusiastic)

PALM TREE (2)

ROCK (2)

FISHERMAN (leading role; energetic, enthusiastic; strong voice)

RIPPLING RIVER (2)

NET (3)

WEAVER (leading role; strong voice; energetic, dramatic)

KENTE CLOTH (3)

SERVANT (authoritative bodyguard)

CHIEF'S CEREMONIAL DRESSER (2)

STOOL BEARER (efficient)

UMBRELLA BEARER (follows Chief wherever he goes)

CHIEF (commanding, imperious)

GOLDEN CEREMONIAL STOOL (3)

All performers, including Sound Crew and Storytellers, can participate in Chorus; in this capacity, everyone does the Chorus actions and chants vigorously, as indicated in the script.

Adaptations You may wish to have one student play the role of both the Cow and a Palm Tree; smaller groups may present the play with only one Yam, Palm Tree, Rock, and so on; one or two students can play all of the Chief's attendants.

Sound Crew

SOUND CREW 1   taped African dance music, triangle, drum, rattle
SOUND CREW 2   bass drum, rattle
SOUND CREW 3   drum, tambourine, rattle
SOUND CREW 4   drum, rattle, jingle bells
SOUND CREW 5   drum, cow bell, rattle, jingle bells
SOUND CREW 6   drum, wood block, rattle

Optional sound effects   Actors and Storytellers can all make sounds using rattles made from objects found around the house. See Chapter Two, *Setting the Scene,* for details. Rattles may be covered with African-style cloths or designs. Performers use the rattles during the opening and closing of the play to accompany taped African music.

Basic Stage Setup

The actors sit on stage in chairs arranged in a semicircle in view of the audience. Costumes and props are stored under the actors' chairs and put on after the opening dance.

The Sound Crew sits with instruments on a table to the right of the stage area, in view of the audience. The tables are set so that the Crew can see the stage.

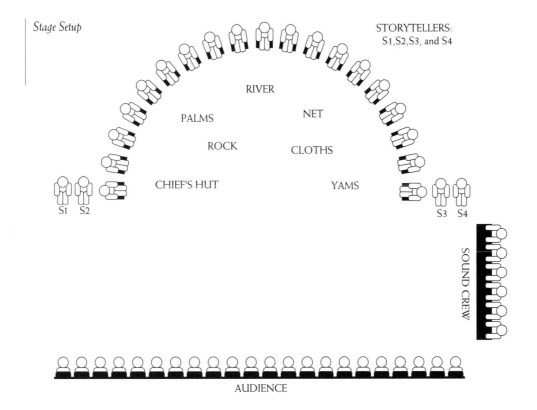

SOUND CREW 1 *plays taped African dance music (see* Production Notes *for suggestions), or the Sound Crew plays drums. Performers can participate in the dance, move in their chairs to the music, or shake rattles to blend in with the music but not overpower it. It is important that everyone move, dance, or play to create the communal African theatre experience. (See* Production Notes *for simple dance steps.)*

After the dance, SOUND CREW 1 *fades out the music, and* STORYTELLER 1 *begins speaking.*

Scene One

Characters   Storytellers, Farmer, Yams, Cow, Dog, Palm Trees

STORYTELLER 1 (*energetically waving*): *Jambo.* Good morning students, adults, too.

STORYTELLER 2: Today we'll do a show for you.

STORYTELLER 3: It is a West African tale, and it is old, yet new.

STORYTELLER 4 (*opening arms wide*): We'll make it come alive for you.

STORYTELLER 1 (*pointing*): So sit right here and have some fun.

STORYTELLER 2 (*gesturing toward heart*): We hope you like it, everyone.

STORYTELLER 3: This West African tale is called...

CHORUS (*emphatically, like a drum beat*): Talk, Talk, Talk.

> (SOUND CREW 2 *and* SOUND CREW 3 *strike rapid drum beats.*)

STORYTELLER 4: It tells of things that like to squawk.

> (SOUND CREW 2 *strikes one emphatic bass drum beat.*)

STORYTELLER 1 (*making a big gesture toward self*): Let it come.

CHORUS (*making a big gesture toward self*): Let it come.

STORYTELLER 2 (*gesturing away from self*): Let it go.

CHORUS: (*gesturing away from self*): Let it go.

STORYTELLER 3: A tale of fun.

STORYTELLER 4: That's never slow.

STORYTELLER 1: Once a farmer was digging up yams in his garden.

> (FARMER *moves to center stage and digs vigorously;* YAMS *kneel, hiding their heads and hands as if underground.*)

CHORUS (*digging with arms*): Dig, dig, dig, dig, dig, dig.

STORYTELLER 2: He pushed the shovel deep.

CHORUS (*digging with arms*): DIG!

STORYTELLER 3: And heard...

YAM 1 (*annoyed*): Ouch.

YAM 2 (*more annoyed, higher voice*): OUCH!

Developing Scripts for Myths and Tales

STORYTELLER 4: The farmer looked around.

(FARMER *scans audience.*)

STORYTELLER 1: He saw nothing and began digging again.

CHORUS (*enthusiastically*): Dig, dig, dig, dig, dig, dig.

STORYTELLER 2: Then he heard an angry sound...

YAM 1 (*angry*): Stop!

YAM 2 (*angrier, louder, more emphatic*): STOP!

(SOUND CREW 6 *hits wood block twice, emphasizing each "stop."*)

STORYTELLER 3: The farmer called his cow.

(FARMER *gestures toward* COW.)

COW (*lumbering; eyes open wide; deep, heavy voice*): Moo. Moo. Moo.

(SOUND CREW 5 *strikes cow bell to accent each "moo."*)

FARMER: Did you talk?

STORYTELLER 4: The cow stared ahead and mooed louder.

COW: Moo.

(SOUND CREW 5 *strikes cow bell.*)

STORYTELLER 1: Then the dog barked and bounced up.

(SOUND CREW 6 *taps wood block in rhythm of bouncing.*)

DOG (*pointing excitedly*): Woof, woof, woof. It was the yams. The yams said, "Stop digging me up."

STORYTELLER 2: The farmer glared at the dog.

STORYTELLER 3: The dog had never talked before.

STORYTELLER 4: And the farmer did not like the way the dog talked to him.

STORYTELLER 1: The dog showed no respect.

STORYTELLER 2: The farmer stomped over to two palm trees.

CHORUS (*moving arms and feet as if stomping*): Stomp, stomp, stomp, stomp.

(SOUND CREW 3 *thumps drum for stomping.*)

STORYTELLER 3: The farmer cut off two fronds—one, two.

(SOUND CREW 6 *taps wood block for each cut.*)

STORYTELLER 4: But the palm trees shook their fronds.

PALM TREE 1 (*pointing at* FARMER): Don't hit that dog.

(SOUND CREW 1–6 *shake rattles.*)

PALM TREE 2 (*pointing*): Don't hit that dog.

(SOUND CREW 1–6 *shake rattles.*)

STORYTELLER 1: The farmer's eyes opened wide.

(FARMER *faces audience, staring;* SOUND CREW 1 *dings triangle.*)

STORYTELLER 2: Talking trees!

(SOUND CREW 1–6 *shake rattles.*)

Scene Two

Characters Storytellers, Farmer, Rocks, River, Fisherman, Yams, Dog, Palm Trees, Net

STORYTELLER 3: There were rocks beside the farmer.

(ROCKS *take position next to* FARMER.)

STORYTELLER 4: The farmer dropped the branches on the rocks—one, two.

(SOUND CREW 6 *strikes wood block for dropping each branch.*)

STORYTELLER 1: But the first rock growled.

ROCK 1 (*raising fist*): Grrr. Don't put that branch on me.

(SOUND CREW 3 *shakes tambourine and slaps it.*)

ROCK 2 (*angrier, raising fist higher*): Grrr. Don't put that branch on me.

(SOUND CREW 3 *shakes tambourine and slaps it.*)

STORYTELLER 3: The talking rocks were too much for the farmer.

STORYTELLER 4: He threw his hands up in the air.

(FARMER *faces audience, throws hands up, and freezes;* SOUND CREW 2 *strikes bass drum emphatically.*)

STORYTELLER 1: His mouth opened wider.

(SOUND CREW 1 *dings triangle.*)

STORYTELLER 2: He began to...

CHORUS (*pumping arms as if running*): *Run,* run, run, run. *Run,* run, run, run. *Run,* run, run, run.

(*Chant is like a drum beat with the accent on the first "run" in each line;* SOUND CREW 1–6 *accompany with muffled drum beats.* FARMER *mimes running in place.*)

STORYTELLER 1 and CHORUS (*thrusting fists forward and freezing*): RUN!

(SOUND CREW 2 *strikes bass drum on final "run."*)

STORYTELLER 2: The farmer came to a rippling river.

RIVER and CHORUS (*rippling arms and shoulders*): Ripple, ripple, ripple, ripple.

(SOUND CREW 4 *and* SOUND CREW 5 *ring jingle bells for rippling.*)

STORYTELLER 3: A fisherman came striding along with a fish net.

(FISHERMAN *strides across stage.* NET *follows, each character holding up a piece of the net.*)

CHORUS (*swinging arms*): Stride, stride, stride, stride.

(SOUND CREW 6 *taps wood block for striding.*)

STORYTELLER 4: The fisherman put up a hand.

(FISHERMAN *points to* FARMER; SOUND CREW 3 *strikes drum.*)

FISHERMAN (*examining the* FARMER): What's the matter with you?

STORYTELLER 1: The farmer pointed back.

(As FARMER *describes everything that talked, each thing stands briskly and repeats excitedly what it said, taking a character stance position.*)

FARMER (*enthusiastically digging*): I was digging yams, and they said...

YAMS (*together, holding up hands*): Stop, stop.

(SOUND CREW 6 *strikes wood block on each "stop."*)

FARMER: My dog said...

DOG (*holding up paws*): Stop digging those yams.

(SOUND CREW 2 *strikes bass drum.*)

FARMER (*higher voice*): The palm trees said...

PALM TREES (*shaking fingers*): Don't hit that dog.

(SOUND CREW 1–6 *shake rattles.*)

FARMER: And the rocks said...

ROCKS (*raising fists*): Grrr. Don't put that branch on me.

(SOUND CREW 3 *shakes tambourine and slaps it.*)

FISHERMAN (*throwing hands up*): Ha, ha, ha, ha.

(SOUND CREW 3 *shakes tambourine for laughing.*)

CHORUS (*throwing hands up*): Ha, ha, ha, ha.

(SOUND CREW 3 *shakes tambourine for laughing.*)

FISHERMAN (*pointing at head*): Are you crazy? Things don't talk.

STORYTELLER 2: But then the net wiggled and said...

NET 1 (*wiggling net a little*): Did he put the branch down?

(SOUND CREW 4 *and* SOUND CREW 5 *shake jingle bells.*)

STORYTELLER 3: The fisherman dropped the net.

Developing Scripts for Myths and Tales

(SOUND CREW 2 *strikes bass drum;* FISHERMAN *drops net in shock; the net falls over, covering the* NET *actors, who freeze.*)

STORYTELLER 4: The fisherman threw his hands up in the air. The farmer threw his hands up in the air.

(FISHERMAN *and* FARMER *face audience—hands up, eyes and mouths open;* SOUND CREW 2 *strikes bass drum as each throws hands up.*)

STORYTELLER 1: They lifted their knees and began to...

CHORUS (*pretending to run*): Run, run, run, run. *Run, run, run, run. Run,* run, run, run.

(*During chant,* FARMER *and* FISHERMAN *circle stage once, running and pumping arms to signify going a distance. They freeze on the final "run," hands thrust forward, facing audience.*)

CHORUS (*thrusting arms forward emphatically*): RUN!

Scene Three

Characters Storytellers, Weaver, Farmer, Fisherman, Kente Cloths, Yams, Dog, Palm Trees, Rocks, Net

STORYTELLER 2: A weaver skipped by with cloth.

(WEAVER *skips across stage energetically.* KENTE CLOTH *actors walk behind, each holding up a cloth.*)

CHORUS (*making energetic skipping motion with arms*): Skip, skip, skip, skip.

(SOUND CREW 1–6 *shake rattles for skipping.*)

STORYTELLER 3: The weaver held up a hand.

WEAVER (*pointing excitedly*): What's the matter with you two?

STORYTELLER 4: The farmer clutched his throat.

(FARMER *grabs at throat.*)

STORYTELLER 1: The fisherman grabbed his head. The farmer began to tell his story.

(FISHERMAN *puts hands to head. As* FARMER *describes everything that talked, each thing stands briskly and repeats excitedly what it said, taking a character stance position.*)

FARMER (*digging excitedly*): I was digging yams, and my yams said...

YAMS (*holding up hands*): Stop, stop.

(SOUND CREW 6 *strikes wood block on each "stop."*)

FARMER: My dog said...

DOG (*holding up paws*): Stop digging those yams.

(SOUND CREW 2 *strikes bass drum.*)

FARMER: The palm trees said...

PALM TREES (*shaking fingers*): Don't hit that dog.

(SOUND CREW 1–6 *shake rattles.*)

FARMER: The rocks said...

ROCKS (*raising fists*): Grrr. Don't put that branch on me.

(SOUND CREW 3 *shakes tambourine and slaps it.*)

STORYTELLER 2: The fisherman continued the story.

FISHERMAN (*pointing to* NET, *excitedly*): My net wiggled...

NET (*wiggling*): Did he put the branch down?

(SOUND CREW 4 *and* SOUND CREW 5 *shake jingle bells.*)

STORYTELLER 3: The weaver laughed.

WEAVER (*throwing hands up*): Ha, ha, ha, ha.

(SOUND CREW 3 *shakes tambourine for laughing.*)

CHORUS (*throwing hands up*): Ha, ha, ha, ha.

(SOUND CREW 3 *shakes tambourine for laughing.*)

WEAVER (*pointing to head*): Are you *crazy?* Things don't *talk!*

STORYTELLER 4: But the cloths popped up and said...

KENTE CLOTH 1 (*popping head above cloth*): Why is he crazy?

(SOUND CREW 6 *taps wood block twice rapidly.*)

KENTE CLOTH 2 (*popping head above cloth; higher voice*): Why is he crazy?

(SOUND CREW 6 *taps wood block twice rapidly.*)

KENTE CLOTH 3 (*popping head above cloth; highest voice*): I don't think he's crazy!

(SOUND CREW 6 *taps wood block twice rapidly.*)

STORYTELLER 1: The weaver jumped back.

(SOUND CREW 1 *thumps drum as* WEAVER *jumps in shock.*)

STORYTELLER 2: The cloths fell in a heap.

(SOUND CREW 3 *thumps drum as the cloths fall together, covering the* CLOTH *actors, who freeze.*)

STORYTELLER 3: The weaver's eyes opened wide.

(WEAVER *faces audience and stares;* SOUND CREW 1 *dings triangle.*)

STORYTELLER 4: The farmer, the fisherman, and the weaver pointed toward the chief's hut.

WEAVER (*pointing excitedly; high voice*): We better tell the chief.

FISHERMAN (*pointing excitedly; higher voice*): The chief, the chief.

FARMER (*pointing excitedly; highest voice*): The chief, the chief, the chief.

STORYTELLER 1: The three began to...

CHORUS (*arms pumping*): *Run,* run, run, run. *Run,* run, run, run. *Run,* run, run, run.

   (*During chant,* FARMER, FISHERMAN, *and* WEAVER *circle stage once, running and pumping arms to signify going a distance. They freeze on the final "run," standing erect with arms thrust forward at shoulder-level.*)

CHORUS (*thrusting arms out shoulder-level*): RUN!

Scene Four

Characters Storytellers, Servant, Farmer, Fisherman, Weaver, Yams, Dog, Palm Trees, Rocks, Net, Kente Cloths, Chief, Chief's Ceremonial Dressers, Umbrella Bearer, Stool Bearer, Stools

STORYTELLER 2: A servant was guarding the chief's hut.

SERVANT (*gesturing to oncoming characters; very sternly*): Stop, stop. What's the matter with you?

FARMER (*excitedly; high voice*): We must see the chief.

FISHERMAN (*excitedly; higher voice*): The chief, the chief.

FARMER (*excitedly; highest voice*): The chief! The chief! The chief!

STORYTELLER 3: The servant strode to the chief. The chief stood with his feet apart and his hands on his hips.

SERVANT (*officially*): There is an emergency.

STORYTELLER 4: The chief was dressed in his ceremonial outfit.

   (SOUND CREW 3 *strikes drum lightly as* CHIEF'S CEREMONIAL DRESSERS *dress* CHIEF; DRESSER 1 *dresses him in African wrap tunic.* DRESSER 2 *hands him a golden staff; elaborate golden pendant could be hung around his neck.*)

STORYTELLER 1: The chief strode out. His umbrella bearer followed him.

   (SOUND CREW 4 *thumps drum for striding.* UMBRELLA BEARER *accompanies* CHIEF, *making sure the umbrella covers the* CHIEF *at all times.*)

STORYTELLER 2: The chief paraded in front of the farmer, fisherman, and weaver with his arms across his chest.

   (SOUND CREW 4 *thumps drum stronger for parading.* CHIEF *moves authoritatively to stand in front of the three characters.*)

STORYTELLER 3: The chief called for his ceremonial stool.

CHIEF (*snapping fingers*): Bring me my golden ceremonial stool.

   (STOOL BEARER *followed by* STOOL *go to center stage.*)

Developing Scripts for Myths and Tales

STORYTELLER 4: The chief sat slowly on the stool.

(SOUND CREW 4 *thumps drum as* CHIEF *walks to* STOOL *and* SOUND CREW 2 *thumps bass drum as* CHIEF *pretends to sit.*)

CHIEF (*domineeringly*): What is the emergency?

(*As* FARMER, FISHERMAN, *and* WEAVER *describe everything that talked, each thing stands briskly and repeats excitedly what it said, taking a character stance position.*)

FARMER (*digging; excitedly*): I was digging up yams, and my yams said...
YAMS (*holding up hands*): Stop. Stop.

(SOUND CREW 6 *strikes wood block on each* "stop.")

FARMER: My dog said...
DOG (*holding up paws*): Stop digging those yams.

(SOUND CREW 2 *strikes bass drum.*)

FARMER: The Palm Trees said...
PALM TREES (*shaking fingers*): Don't hit that dog.

(SOUND CREW 1–6 *shake rattles.*)

FARMER: The rocks said...
ROCKS (*raising fists*): Grrr. Don't put that branch on me.

(SOUND CREW 3 *shakes tambourine and slaps it.*)

FISHERMAN (*pointing to* NET *excitedly*): The net wiggled...
NET (*wiggling*): Did he put the branch down?

(SOUND CREW 4 *and* SOUND CREW 5 *shake jingle bells.*)

WEAVER (*pointing to* KENTE CLOTHS *excitedly*): The cloth said...
KENTE CLOTHS (*popping up heads*): I don't think he's crazy.

(SOUND CREW 6 *taps wood block twice.*)

CHIEF (*jumping up, facing audience, showing teeth; pointing to other characters*): What nonsense! You think things talk. Get out of here before I arrest you.
STORYTELLER 1: The three jumped back.

(SOUND CREW 1 *thumps drum.*)

STORYTELLER 2: They waved their hands.

(*The* FARMER, FISHERMAN, *and* WEAVER *face the other actors, waving arms.* CHORUS *waves arms, too;* SOUND CREW 3 *shakes tambourine and* SOUND CREW 4–6 *shake rattles.*)

STORYTELLER 3: They headed toward the bush and they began to...
CHORUS: *Run*, run, run. run. *Run*, run, run, run. *Run*, run, run, run.

(FARMER, FISHERMAN, *and* WEAVER *run to their chairs with their backs to audience, running in place until the final "run."*)

CHORUS (*freezing, arms thrust forward*): RUN!

STORYTELLER 1: The chief glanced at his stool and growled.

CHIEF (*to audience*): Grrr. That kind of talk disturbs the community.

STORYTELLER 2: The chief glared.

(CHIEF *glares at audience.*)

STORYTELLER 3: But just then the stool squawked...

STOOL 1 (*head up*): You're right.

STOOL 2 (*head up; higher voice*): Yes, you're right.

STOOL 3 (*head up, waving ceremonial staff, highest voice*): Whoever heard of a talking *yam*?

STORYTELLER 4: The chief jumped four feet up in the air.

(CHIEF *faces audience and jumps as high as possible;* SOUND CREW 2 *strikes bass drum.*)

STORYTELLER 1: He stared at the stool.

(CHIEF *stares in disbelief.*)

STORYTELLER 2: He waved his arms wildly and shouted...

CHIEF (*waving frantically and in high voice*): HELP! HELP!

STORYTELLER 3: And he began to...

CHORUS: *Run, run, run, run. Run, run, run, run. Run, run, run, run.*

(CHIEF *circles stage pumping and waving arms wildly.*)

CHORUS: *RUN!*

(On the final "run," SOUND CREW 1–6 pound drum once in unison. The CHIEF stands frozen in center stage with hands held up high and eyes opened wide. Everyone should give the CHIEF a surprised look.)

STORYTELLER 4: (*pointing at chief*): That was our story of...

CHORUS: Talk, Talk, Talk.

STORYTELLER 1: That tells of things that like to squawk.

STORYTELLER 2 (*gesturing to self*): Let it come.

CHORUS (*gesturing to self*): Let it come.

STORYTELLER 3 (*gesturing away from self*): Let it go.

CHORUS (*gesturing away from self*): Let it go.

STORYTELLER 4: A tale of fun.

STORYTELLER 1: That's never slow.

(SOUND CREW 1 *plays taped African dance music, or the* SOUND CREW *plays drums. Performers may do the same dance steps as in the beginning of the play or improvise and do some variations of the movements. Audience may be asked to clap along or even to dance. After a while* SOUND CREW 1 *fades the music for the play's finale.*)

Finale

(STORYTELLERS *should memorize only this short part so that they can go center stage and recite it.*)

STORYTELLER 1: Thank you students, adults, too.

STORYTELLER 2: For watching so kindly our show for you.

STORYTELLER 3: Of a West African tale, old yet new.

STORYTELLER 4: We hope it came alive for you.

STORYTELLER 1: And here's a last tip from us, your friends.

STORYTELLER 2 (*holding up a colorful picture book with an African tale*): Read a book of these tales from beginning to end.

STORYTELLER 3: And study different cultures wherever they may be.

STORYTELLER 4: For the more that you know, the more you'll be...

(STORYTELLERS *gesture to all performers.*)

EVERYONE (*making big circular gesture around their heads*): Free!

STORYTELLER 1: The actors are...

STORYTELLER 2: The sound crew is...

STORYTELLER 3: The storytellers are...

STORYTELLER 4: Thank you for coming to our play.

To end the performance, STORYTELLERS 1—4 *introduce the performers, having them stand and say their names loudly and clearly. When all are standing,* STORYTELLERS 1—4 *turn toward them and raise arms. Everyone follows, raising their arms and bringing them down together for a bow. Performers then sit for the audience performance discussion.*

Story Questions and Research Topics

To spark students' interest and enrich the cultural experience, provide a variety of materials for investigation, dramatic play, study, and observation. Suggestions include artifacts, clothing, utensils, photographs, artwork, and books. Discussion questions and research topics can be pursued before embarking on a drama experience, during play rehearsal, or after the production to support the culture being introduced.

Story Questions

1. What is the funniest thing that happens in the story? Why do you think so?

2. Who is your favorite character? Why?

3. Who is the funniest character? Why do you think so?

4. This story is called a *cumulative tale,* meaning that the things that happen grow or accumulate. What grows or accumulates in this story?

5. Things in this story talk. Of course, things do not actually talk in real life, but sometimes they seem to act badly and talk back. Give an example of something you own or someone you know owns that misbehaves and even seems to talk back at times. Find other stories in which things talk. How do the things feel about people?

6. Some African stories were used to keep chiefs from feeling too high and mighty. What happens in this story that might teach the chief a lesson? Why might the chief in this story need to learn a lesson?

7. Traditionally in Africa, chiefs would not conduct business unless they were sitting on their sacred stools. Why, then, is it particularly funny that the chief's stool talks back?

8. Stories and plays often build to a climax, a moment that is the most exciting. What is the climactic or most exciting moment in this story?

9. This story takes place in Ghana in West Africa. Ghanaians respect all life and nature. How do people treat things in this story? What might be the moral or lesson of this story?

Theater-Performance Questions

1. African theatre tries to create a special, close bond with the audience, making them a part of the play and giving them a chance to participate in a production. What is the value of this participation for an audience and for the performers? What might you as a performer do to create a bond with your audience?

2. Many consider dancing to be an important African art. Dancers often improvise steps. What does *improvise* mean? Where have you seen examples of improvised dance?

3. An African dance expert has said that in Africa, dance is used to express a person's inner life and experience. How might a dance express what people feel or imagine inside? How does this make dancing valuable?

4. African theatre emphasizes exaggerated mime—finding the essential part of an action and acting it out clearly and vigorously. What actions mimed by characters in this play should be done with exaggerated emphasis to show the excitement of the drama?

5. Storytellers in African theatre try to embody the characters through gestures, facial expressions, and voice intonations. What does *embodying the characters* mean? Why is this a good storytelling technique?

6. African music tries to express life in all its aspects. Thus, some sounds might be harsh, like splitting stones with a pick. What other sounds in nature or in daily life would require a harsh sound effect?

Research Topics

1. This story takes place in Accra, Ghana's capital. It became the capital of the Gold Coast in 1877. Find Ghana on a map. Why is Ghana called the Gold Coast? Where is gold mentioned in this play?

2. This play features a farmer, fisherman, and weaver. Study Ghana's culture. Why might an audience in Ghana be particularly interested in those professions?

3. Kente cloth is popular in the United States. It is imported from Ghana. What is kente cloth? How is it made? What is distinctive about it?

4. The chief's stool is as important to Africans as a monarch's throne is in European cultures. The stool of the chief of the Ashanti in Ghana is golden. It is common for people other than a chief to have a special stool, too. Find out why the stool is considered to be so important.

5. Yams are Ghana's most important crop. There is a sacred yam festival. What other culture represented in this book finds a crop sacred?

6. All cultures give special attention to their heads of state. Describe cultures you know about and the special treatment they give their heads of state. What special treatment does the President of the United States receive? What might be the value of special treatment for heads of state?

7. The drum is the most important African instrument. If there is no drum, people clap, stamp, or repeat words rhythmically. Where in this play are these techniques used? What effect is created? Why are the best dancers those who best follow the drum?

8. Drums are made of a variety of materials and come in different shapes and sizes. Why might drummers want to have many kinds of drums? Research different types of drums and how they are made.

9. Many cultures use the drum for entertainment and for spiritual reasons. Why is drumming so powerful? What makes people respond to it?

Selected Bibliography

Picture Books

Aardema, Verna. *Anansi Finds a Fool.* Illustrated by Bryna. New York: Dial Books for Young Readers, 1992. Tricky Anansi gets tricked himself. Inspiring pictures help students appreciate African fashion and life style.

————. *Traveling to Tondo: A Tale of the Nkundo of Zaire.* Illustrated by Will Hillenbrand. New York: Alfred A. Knopf, 1991. Amusing cumulative story with evocative African pictures; good for all ages to act.

————. *Why Mosquitoes Buzz in People's Ears: A West African Tale.* New York: Dial Books for Young Readers, 1975. This popular book of Mosquito's lie is a natural to dramatize.

————. *Who's in Rabbit's House?* Illustrated by Leo and Diane Dillon. New York: Dial Books for Young Readers, 1977. The Masai story of an invader of Rabbit's House is told like a play, with Africans dressed in masks. Amusing and stimulating; inspires dramatization.

Bryan, Ashley. *Beat the Story-Drum, Pum-Pum.* New York: Atheneum, 1987. Five Nigerian action tales told in rhythmic language; good to dramatize. Illustrated with woodcuts.

Haley, Gail. *A Story—A Story.* New York: Atheneum, 1970. Caldecott winner about trickster hero Anansi, with colorful, authentic African woodcuts.

Mendez, Philip. *The Black Snowman.* Illustrated by Carole Byard. New York: Scholastic, Inc., 1989. A poignant story of a boy's magical boost of esteem when his snowman receives life through an African storyteller's kente cloth. Excellent to dramatize.

Steptoe, John. *Mufario's Beautiful Daughter: An African Tale.* New York: Lothrop, Lee and Shepard, 1987. A moving African Cinderella tale, with beautiful pictures depicting ruins of an ancient city in Zimbabwe.

Collections

Abrahams, Roger D., ed. *Afro-American Folktales: Stories from Black Traditions in the New World.* New York: Pantheon Books, 1985. Fifty-two authentic tales that appeal to older students grouped into amusing categories such as *Minding Somebody Else's Business* and *Getting a Comeuppance.*

Courlander, Harold, and George Herzog. *Cow-Tail Switch and Other West African Stories.* New York: Henry Holt, 1947. Seventeen stories with background notes for each. Includes a version of *Talk, Talk, Talk.*

————. *Olode the Hunter and Other Tales from Nigeria.* San Diego: Harcourt Brace and World, 1963. Another good collection of authentic African tales.

Hamilton, Virginia. *The People Could Fly.* Illustrated by Leo and Diane Dillon. New York: Alfred A. Knopf, 1985. Folk tales told by slaves, divided into categories such as animal tales, tales of the supernatural, and slave tales of freedom. Each has historical background information.

Sherlock. Philip M. *Anansi, the Spider Man.* New York: Thomas Y. Crowell, 1954. Delightful trickster stories for ages nine and above.

Cultural Information

Hintz, Martin. *Enchantment of the World: Ghana.* Chicago: Children's Press, 1987. Easy to read, colorful, informative, and appealing.

Musgrove, Margaret. *Ashanti to Zulu: African Traditions.* Illustrated by Leo and Diane Dillon. New York: Dial Books for Young Readers, 1976. Brilliantly illustrated alphabet book showing traditions of twenty-six African tribes. Winner of the 1976 Caldecott Medal.

Theater and Performance

Jones, Bessie, and Bess Lomax Hawes. *Step it Down: Games, Plays, Songs and Stories from Afro-American Heritage.* New York: Harper and Row, 1972. These authentic games, plays, chants, and claps will delight all age levels.

Serwadda, W. Moses. *Songs and Stories from Uganda.* Transcribed and edited by Hewitt Pantaleoni. Illustrated by Leo and Diane Dillon. New York: Thomas Y. Crowell Company, 1974. Thirteen stories and songs that go with them showing how music, story, and performance are integrated in African culture.

Warren, Lee. *The Dance of Africa: An Introduction.* Englewood Cliffs, NJ: Prentice Hall, 1972. Shows how dance relates to the total life style of Africans. Describes representative dances.

———. *The Theater of Africa.* Englewood Cliffs, NJ: Prentice Hall, 1975. Shows how traditional African drama is integrated into African religions and customs. Excellent background.

CHAPTER SIX

The Creation and the Birth of the Corn God
A Mayan Creation Myth

𝕏𝕏 ◉ 𝕏𝕏

This myth of how the world was created is similar in both the Mayan and Aztec cultures. Both the Mayans and Aztecs believe that the gods made several attempts at creation before the present world was formed, and both believe that corn is the flesh and blood of people.

The Mayan version was written down by Spanish friars who transcribed oral accounts of the gods given to them by the Mayans. The friars also translated the Mayan holy religious book of legend and history, the Popol Vuh. This play is based on these records.

In the beginning, there was only water. The Sun God and Moon Goddess called *Earth*, and land appeared. The gods filled the land with trees and animals. But the animals could not praise the gods properly. So the gods tried creating people, because people would be able to praise the gods. First they formed people from mud, but Mud People were too wobbly to show praise for the Sun God and Moon Goddess. The Mud People soaked up water and dissolved. The Sun God and Moon Goddess tried making people from wood, but Wood People were too rigid and heartless to show praise for their creation. Dogs, pots, a grinding stone, trees, rain, and a cave all objected to the Wood People, who ran into the forest to escape. These rigid Wood People are the ancestors of monkeys. The Sun God and Moon Goddess became down-hearted because they could not create people who would praise them. So a Magic Grandmother used ears of corn to form Corn People, and these Corn People praised the Sun God and Moon Goddess for giving them life. When a Corn God emerged from under a large rock, the Corn People had a god to worship, and they performed a dance in the Corn God's honor.

Acting Exercises

The following acting exercises may be used to help students practice acting principles and develop the characters that make up the cast of this play.

Becoming the Moon Goddess or Sun God

Goal To use voice and stance to convey authority and power.

Acting Principles Belief, Voice and Movement.

Procedure Divide the class into Group One and Group Two. Each group does every other one of the following exercises. In each exercise, students take turns acting the role of the Moon Goddess or the Sun God. Groups comment on each other's believable acting and on the students' use of voice and movement to create the characters of the Moon Goddess and Sun God.

- Become the Moon Goddess or Sun God. Stand regally, showing you can lead and command the world. Freeze.
- Stretch forth your arm powerfully and call Earth and Life to form. Freeze.
- Regally say "Welcome" to the Earth and Life you have created.
- Authoritatively banish the animals that did not praise you, saying "Go to your homes." Freeze.

Character Transformation With Sound Effects

Goal To coordinate voice, movement, and control with sound effects.

Acting Principles Belief, Voice and Movement, Control.

Procedure Actors stand to assume the role of a character from the following list of roles. Each actor should take a character stance, coordinating movement with sound effect as indicated. The sound crew plays the effect given in parentheses.

- Rippling Sea (triangle)
- Swirling Mists (jingle bells and wind chimes)
- Mountain (triangle)
- Cedar and Pine Tree (wood block) Begin as seeds tucked up on ground; on slow count of five, grow into trees with outstretched branches.
- Prancing Deer (wood block)
- Swooping Orange Bird (bell) "Tweet, tweet, tweet."
- Pawing Jaguar (drum) "Roar, roar, roar."
- Slithering Serpent (guiro) "Hiss, hiss, hiss."
- Shaking Ceiba Tree (rattles)
- Snarling Dogs (no sound effect) "You never fed me."
- Snarling Dogs (no sound effect) "You never played with me."
- Threatening Burned Pots (gong) "You burn me."
- Howling Grinding Stone (guiro) "You grind, grind, grind me."

Molding and Becoming Mud People

Goal To use pantomime to act out the creation of the Mud People.

Acting Principle Belief.

Procedure Divide the class into two groups. Students in Group One become the Sun God or Moon Goddess molding Mud People; students in Group Two are the Mud People they create. A list of steps for each activity is provided below. Have the groups trade roles. Groups comment on each other's miming and believable acting.

- God or Goddess molding a Mud Person:

  Look down and discover a clump of cool, wet mud.

  Pick it up. Test its consistency. It is just right for molding.

  Mold a head and neck. Put in details of a face.

  Mold strong shoulders and arms.

  Mold a narrow waist.

  Mold two long, powerful legs.

  Mold two big feet to hug the earth.

  Freeze. Examine your creation. Does it need more?

- Mud Person being molded by a God or Goddess:

  You are a clump of cool, wet mud.

  Slowly you feel your head and neck being molded. Show your eyes, nose, and mouth being formed.

  Show how your wide shoulders, strong arms, and waist are molded.

  Experience first one long, strong leg being molded and then another.

  You are wobbly when you stand.

  Rain comes. Feel it soaking all through your mud body. Your mouth gapes open, your back slumps, your legs disintegrate, and you slowly dissolve back into a clump of mud. Freeze.

Carving and Becoming Wood People

Goal To use pantomime to act out the creation of the Wood People.

Acting Principles Belief.

Procedure Divide the class into two groups. Students in Group One become the Sun God or Moon Goddess whittling Wood People; students in Group Two are the Wood People they create. A list of steps for each activity is provided below. Have the groups trade roles. Groups comment on each other's miming and believable acting.

- God or Goddess whittling a Wood Person:

  Find a tall tree stump. Pick up a heavy knife with a strong blade.

  Carve a head. Show the details of the face. The wood is tough and hard and takes effort to carve.

  Carve a neck and shoulders. You may need another instrument to help you carve that tough wood.

  Chisel two long arms. Whittle a narrow waist.

Carve one long leg and then another. Chisel two big feet so that the people can stand firmly on the ground.

- Wood Person being molded by a God or Goddess:

  You are a rigid tree stump.

  Slowly you feel your stiff wooden head being whittled. The carver forms stiff wooden eyes and a stiff mouth.

  Show how the wood is whittled away to form your rigid neck.

  Rigid shoulders are formed slowly—first one, then the other.

  One stiff wooden arm juts out and then another.

  The carver whittles a waist. Here comes one rigid leg and then another.

  Finally there is one big, flat, wood foot and then another.

  Freeze and stare woodenly. Raise a wooden hand and say "Hola" in a loud, rigid, wooden voice.

Becoming Destructive, Angry Rain

Goal   To use voice and movement to convey the force of a storm.

Acting Principles   Belief, Control, Voice and Movement.

Procedure   Tell students they will become the Rain trying to destroy the heartless Wood People. Discuss the need to create exciting, dynamic, jagged rain artistically and with control. Half of the class acts using the following instructions while the other half observes, commenting on controlled artistic acting. Then trade roles.

- Stand and freeze in a jagged rain shape.
- Move up, down, and all around, occupying your own territory to create rain that will destroy the heartless Wood People.
- Freeze in a powerful, threatening, jagged rain shape, showing your goal with your whole face and body.

Production Notes

The following guidelines may be used to enhance the quality of the production with dance movements and simple costumes.

Mayan Creation and Corn God Dance

Music   "Sombrero de Paja y Quina," from the audio tape entitled *Andes Manta*, played by Wilson Lopez, Luis Lopez, Bolivar Lopez, Acrolos Armas, and Fernando Moya de Quito, 1992. Koch International Corporation, 122 Cantiague Rock Road, Westbury, NY, 11590. (Any other instrumental music of Central America would be suitable.)

Purpose and Style   To seek help from and show respect to the gods.

Materials   Students might beat sticks (made of foot-long dowels) as they dance. A few might play bells and rattles. Sound Crew plays drums and rattles, blending in with the taped music.

The lead dancer wears a ceremonial paper bag headdress covered with feathers and bright fabrics, and carries two feather dusters. Others might also wear ceremonial hats. (See *Costumes and Fabrics*, Chapter Two, and any additional pictures of Mayan headdresses which are available.)

Formation   A circle moving in a clockwise direction.

Steps and Stances   Small, restrained steps; the foot is hardly lifted off the ground. Arms move up and down rhythmically.

> *Step One:* Lead dancer stands upstage center holding feather dusters above head to signal music to begin; performers sit in their chairs in a semicircle around the leader. Music begins and leader, taking small steps, raises and lowers feather dusters, moving to down center. Reaching down center, leader turns toward performers, raises dusters up, and freezes, signaling performers to rise.

Step One

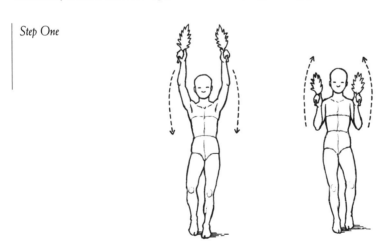

Step Two: Performers stand and raise sticks or other instruments to show they are ready to begin. Leader turns clockwise. Performers follow. All performers do the leader's first step, playing instruments and lifting them up and down as they circle the stage area twice.

Step Three: Leader stops in starting position (down center), raises dusters up, and freezes. Dancers freeze with their hands up. Leader circles in place twice. Dancers follow.

Step Three

Step Four: Leader moves to center of the circle, raising arms up. Dancers do the same. Leader moves out, lowering arms; dancers follow. The movement is repeated, in and out four times.

Leader freezes, holding arms up; dancers freeze, too. The leader turns clockwise, and all the dancers do the same step to their seats. Music fades when last dancer sits. Actors put on costume pieces, and Storyteller One begins the first lines of the play, speaking in an enthusiastic voice to grab the audience's attention.

Finale: The final dance to honor the Corn God at the conclusion of the play is the same as the opening dance, except that the four Corn People raise and lower ears of corn (instead of instruments) as they dance. The Corn God stands at center stage, frozen in a gesture of offering corn to the people, as the dancers circle around with their heads moving up and down to honor the Corn God.

Costume Suggestions

For ceremonies, Mayans wear elaborate, high headdresses with plumes (they worship birds); headdresses may include animal heads or other decoration for theatre and ceremony. (See *Selected Bibliography* for books with good illustrations of such headdresses.)

For narrative mime presentations, all students wear black clothing—black shirts and black pants—with individual character costumes worn as additional pieces to the all-black attire.

Storytellers Brown paper grocery bags can be covered with feathers or plumes made of colored construction paper to create decorative headdresses. Other showy ornaments might be added. Storytellers might wear choir robes or no-sew tunics (see Chapter Two) of the same or different colors to look like priests, who often passed down the teachings of Mayan mythology.

Sun God and Moon Goddess   Make headdresses with stiff cardboard or tagboard. Make them as high as possible, with a silver moon or gold sun on top. Cover the sun and moon with glitter, foil, sequins, or some other material that will be striking from a distance.

Sea   Transparent light blue material extending the length of the stage; can be two to three feet wide.

Mist   Glue or tape long white strips of crepe paper to dowels; use two dowels for each performer.

Mountain   Two dowels or yard sticks (one for each student) to raise on cue; the dowels should be held so that the ends touch and each forms one side of the mountain peak. Alternatively, students can act without costumes, using only their bodies to create a sense of mountains.

Cedar and Pine   Hold real tree branches or make a tunic from green and brown material with a hole cut through it for the head; cut the bottom edge in a jagged shape. (See *Costumes and Fabrics,* Chapter Two.)

Deer   A brown baseball cap with small tree branches attached for antlers.

Orange Bird   Attach orange feathers to a headband or orange baseball cap.

Jaguar   Attach black spots to a yellow baseball cap or animal ears to a paper headpiece. (See *Costumes and Fabrics,* Chapter Two.)

Serpent   A dark green baseball cap worn with the brim in back; attach red felt eyes with fabric glue.

Mud People   Tunic costumes made from mud-colored cloth.

Wood People   Two pieces of light brown or bark-colored cloth, enough to cover the actors when standing.

Rain   Attach silver, gray, and black strips of material to dowels; use two dowels for each performer.

Cave   No costume other than black clothing is necessary. Actors use their bodies to form the rounded shape of a cave.

Ceiba Tree   Green paper or plastic leaves can be held in each hand or made into a wreath and worn on the head.

Dog   Attach ears to baseball caps of appropriate colors or make paper head pieces. (See Chapter Two.)

Pots   Old kitchen pots painted black on the bottom.

Grinding Stone   A shallow box to simulate a grinding stone.

Corn People   Each carries an ear of real or decorative corn.

Grandmother   Brightly colored shawl.

Dawn   Orange netting that extends the length of the stage; can be two to three feet wide.

Golden Light   Attach gold tinsel to two dowels.

Sun   A tunic of bright yellow fabric.

Lake   A piece of light blue fabric, approximately three feet square.

Palm Tree   A green tunic with pointed, stylized palm frond edges. To differentiate Palm from Pine and Cedar, use material with a different color and texture; consider adding a green feather boa, if available.

Rock   Gray material big enough for Corn God to hide behind, approximately one to two yards square.

Thunder God   No costume other than black clothing is necessary.

Corn God   Golden headdress (not a crown) with green material attached for creating locks of hair and to represent the corn leaves. (See *Costumes and Fabrics*, Chapter Two.) Around shoulders, drape a three-foot piece of gold or yellow nylon netting. Ear of corn to be held might have green and gold ribbons tied to it.

XOX ◉ XOX

The Creation and the Birth of the Corn God

A Mayan Creation Myth

Cast

FOUR STORYTELLERS (strong, clear, enthusiastic voices and gestures)

SUN GOD (strong, regal)

MOON GODDESS (strong, regal)

SEA (2)

MIST (3)

MOUNTAIN (2)

CEDAR

PINE

DEER

ORANGE BIRD

JAGUAR

SERPENT

MUD PEOPLE (2)

WOOD PEOPLE (2)

RAIN (3)

CAVE (2)

CEIBA OR SILK COTTON TREE

DOG (2)

POT (2)

GRINDING STONE

CORN PEOPLE (4)

MAGIC GRANDMOTHER

DAWN (2)

GOLDEN LIGHT (2)

SUN

LAKE (2)

PALM TREE

ROCK (2)

THUNDER GOD (4 or more)

GORN GOD (majestic, regal)

Adaptations For smaller groups, a pair of students could portray Sea, Mist, Mountain, Cedar and Pine, Deer, Bird, Jaguar, Serpent; another pair can play Rain, Ceiba Tree, Dog, Pot, Grinding Stone. Use only one Dog and one Pot; mime location of cave.

Sound Crew

SOUND CREW 1   taped music, drum, rattle
SOUND CREW 2   triangle, dinner bell, rattle
SOUND CREW 3   wind chimes, guiro, tambourine, rattle
SOUND CREW 4   slide whistle, gong, rattle
SOUND CREW 5   wood block, sand blocks, rattle
SOUND CREW 6   Piano or resonator bells (does not need to know how to play the piano)

Other instruments may be substituted, added, or made with found objects. Suggestions for making instruments are in Chapter Two.

Basic Stage Setup

The actors sit on stage in chairs arranged in a semicircle in view of the audience. Costumes and props are stored under the actors' chairs and put on after the opening dance. Arrange blue, filmy cloth or scarves downstage to represent Sea.

The Sound Crew sits with instruments on a table to the right of the stage area, in view of the audience. The tables are set so that the Crew can see the stage.

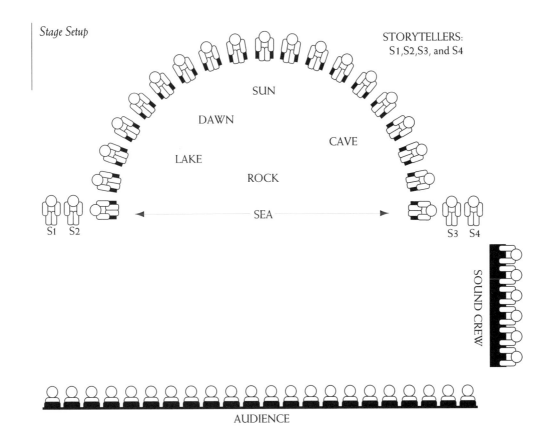

Stage Setup

STORYTELLERS:
S1, S2, S3, and S4

SUN

DAWN

CAVE

LAKE

ROCK

← SEA →

S1   S2   S3   S4

SOUND CREW

AUDIENCE

SOUND CREW 1 *plays taped music and actors and storytellers perform the Mayan dance. (See* Production Notes *for suggested music and dance steps.) After the dance,* SOUND CREW 1 *fades music and* STORYTELLER 1 *begins speaking.*

Scene One

Characters   Storytellers, Moon Goddess, Sun God, Sea, Mist, Mountain, Cedar, Pine, Deer, Bird, Jaguar, Serpent

STORYTELLER 1 (*brightly, enthusiastically*): The creation.

(SOUND CREW 2 *dings triangle.*)

STORYTELLER 2: A Mayan myth of how the world began.

(SOUND CREW 2 *dings triangle.*)

STORYTELLER 3 (*gesturing above stage*): First there was only heaven...

STORYTELLER 4 (*gesturing to Sea*): ...and the sea.

(SEA *actors move downstage, pick up sea cloth, and gently ripple it.* SOUND CREW 2 *dings triangle several times as* SEA *foams and ripples.*)

STORYTELLER 1: Only the Sun God and the Moon Goddess stood majestically in the rippling water.

(*The* GOD *and* GODDESS *walk regally behind* SEA.)

STORYTELLER 2: The Moon Goddess called for Earth.

MOON GODDESS (*enthusiastically, reaching out hand*): Earth.

(SOUND CREW 2 *dings triangle.*)

STORYTELLER 3: The Sun God called for Life.

SUN GOD (*authoritatively, making sweeping gesture*): Life.

(SOUND CREW 2 *dings triangle.*)

STORYTELLER 4: The sea withdrew.

(SEA *moves slowly upstage, rippling; seated actors lift cloth over their heads and drop it inconspicuously behind their chairs.* SOUND CREW 2 *dings triangle several times as* SEA *withdraws.*)

STORYTELLER 1: Mists swirled.

(MIST *actors swirl lightly and gracefully, moving bodies up, down, and all over the stage, taking time to create the effect.* SOUND CREW 2 *jingles bells and* SOUND CREW 3 *jingles wind chimes lightly.* MISTS *return to their seats.*)

STORYTELLER 2: Mountains pushed upward.

(MOUNTAINS *kneel facing each other and slowly begin to stand up, miming the effort of pushing up from the earth; Mountain props may be used to form a mountain peak.* SOUND CREW 2 *strikes triangle twice as peak forms.*)

STORYTELLER 3: Seeds grew into tall, full pines.

(CEDAR *and* PINE *kneel, tucking heads down to become seeds.* SOUND CREW 5 *strikes wood block slowly five times as* CEDAR *and* PINE *stand, growing into trees with outstretched branches.*)

STORYTELLER 4: The Sun God and Moon Goddess welcomed them.

MOON GODDESS (*enthusiastically, reaching arm toward them*): Welcome.

(SOUND CREW 6 *sweeps fingers along high piano notes or strikes mallet along keys of resonator bells.*)

SUN GOD (*exuberantly, reaching arm toward them*): Welcome!

(SOUND CREW 6 *sweeps fingers along high piano notes or strikes mallet along keys of resonator bells.* MOUNTAIN *and* TREES *sit.*)

STORYTELLER 1: They created animals. Prancing Deer...

MOON GODDESS (*echoing* STORYTELLER): Prancing Deer.

(*As each animal is called, it stands and moves forward as described, freezing in a stylized posture.* SOUND CREW 2 *dings triangle as each animal is called.* SOUND CREW 5 *strikes wood block for prancing.*)

STORYTELLER 2: Swooping Orange Bird...

SUN GOD: Swooping Orange Bird.

(SOUND CREW 2 *dings triangle.* SOUND CREW 2 *rings bell for swooping.*)

STORYTELLER 3: Pawing Jaguar...

MOON GODDESS: Pawing Jaguar.

(SOUND CREW 2 *dings triangle.* SOUND CREW 1 *strikes drum for pawing.*)

STORYTELLER 4: Slithering Serpent...

SUN GOD: Slithering Serpent.

(SOUND CREW 2 *dings triangle.* SOUND CREW 3 *scrapes guiro for slithering.*)

STORYTELLER 1: They asked the animals to speak.

MOON GODDESS (*commandingly*): Speak.

SUN GOD (*commandingly*): Speak.

STORYTELLER 2: Orange Bird whistled.

(SOUND CREW 2 *rings bell.* ORANGE BIRD *flaps wings and whistles.*)

STORYTELLER 3: Jaguar roared.

(SOUND CREW 1 *strikes medium drum beats.*)

JAGUAR (*showing teeth and claws*): Roar, roar, roar.

STORYTELLER 4: Serpent hissed.

(SOUND CREW 3 *scrapes guiro.*)

SERPENT (*thrusting neck forward*): Hiss, Hiss, hiss.

STORYTELLER 1: But the animals could not praise them.

MOON GODDESS: We want creatures to praise us.

SUN GOD: Yes, we want creatures to praise us.

STORYTELLER 2: They commanded the animals to go to their homes.

MOON GODDESS (*pointing authoritatively*): Go home.

SUN GOD (*pointing authoritatively*): Go home.

STORYTELLER 3: Deer pranced to the forest.

(SOUND CREW 5 *taps wood block as* DEER *prances lightly back to seat.*)

STORYTELLER 4: Orange Bird flew to a tree.

(SOUND CREW 2 *rings bell as Orange Bird flies back to seat.*)

STORYTELLER 1: Jaguar pawed to the brush.

(SOUND CREW 1 *strikes drum as* JAGUAR *paws back to seat.*)

STORYTELLER 2: Serpent slithered to a cave.

(SOUND CREW 3 *scrapes guiro as* SERPENT *slithers to seat.*)

STORYTELLER 3: They paced back and forth. What should they do now?

Scene Two

Characters   Storytellers, Moon Goddess, Sun God, Mud People

STORYTELLER 4: The Moon Goddess saw a clump of mud.

(MUD PEOPLE *actors kneel, facing audience and holding up brown cloth so that their bodies are concealed. Cloth should remain stationary.* SOUND CREW 6 *strikes several low piano notes.*)

STORYTELLER 1: She suggested making people from mud.

MOON GODDESS (*enthusiastically pointing at mud*): Let's make people from mud.

STORYTELLER 2: They picked up some mud.

(SOUND CREW 6 *strikes low piano notes as mud forms.*)

STORYTELLER 3: They molded a head and neck.

(SOUND CREW 6 *strikes two high piano notes as* SUN GOD *and* MOON GODDESS *carefully mold head and neck.* MUD PEOPLE *move cloth down, showing heads and necks as* SUN GOD *and* MOON GODDESS *mold them.*)

STORYTELLER 4: They molded a waist and arms.

(SOUND CREW 6 *strikes middle piano notes as* SUN GOD *and* MOON GODDESS *mold waist and arms;* MUD PEOPLE *lower cloth as they appear.*)

Developing Scripts for Myths and Tales

STORYTELLER 1: They molded two legs.

(SOUND CREW 6 *strikes two low piano notes after* SUN GOD *and* MOON GODDESS *mold legs and* MUD PEOPLE *appear.*)

STORYTELLER 2: They looked like people, but their heads flopped to the side, and their mouths gaped open.

(SOUND CREW 6 *plays high, floppy piano notes as each of these movements occur.*)

STORYTELLER 3: Their backs slumped.

(SOUND CREW 4 *plays slide whistle.* MUD PEOPLE *slump.*)

STORYTELLER 4: Their legs wobbled.

(SOUND CREW 6 *strikes low piano notes several times for wobbling legs.*)

STORYTELLER 1: They soaked up water and fell apart.

(SOUND CREW 4 *plays slide whistle as* MUD PEOPLE *disintegrate in slow motion.*)

STORYTELLER 2: The Sun God and Moon Goddess shook their heads. Mud People were no good.

(MUD PEOPLE *sit.*)

STORYTELLER 3: They frowned, thinking again.

Scene Three

Characters Storytellers, Sun God, Moon Goddess, Wood People, Rain, Ceiba Tree, Dog, Pot, Grinding Stone

STORYTELLER 4: The Sun God saw two tree stumps.

(SOUND CREW 5 *strikes wood block as each stump forms.* WOOD PEOPLE *stand, covering themselves with wood cloths. They keep cloths stationary and remain stiff to resemble stumps.*)

STORYTELLER 1: The Sun God suggested making Wood People.

SUN GOD: Let's make Wood People.

STORYTELLER 2: They carved a head and neck.

(SOUND CREW 3 *scrapes guiro as* SUN GOD *and* MOON GODDESS *mime carefully carving head and neck.* WOOD PEOPLE *lower cloths to reveal heads and necks.*)

STORYTELLER 3: They carved a waist and arms.

(SOUND CREW 3 *scrapes guiro. Waist is revealed. Arms stretch out woodenly.*)

STORYTELLER 4: They carved two legs.

(SOUND CREW 3 *scrapes guiro. Legs are revealed and cloths drop to ground.*)

STORYTELLER 1: The Wood People walked rigidly.

(SOUND CREW 5 *strikes wood block as* WOOD PEOPLE *parade rigidly to audience, then to each other, and then back.*)

STORYTELLER 2: They said, *Hola, Hello,* rigidly.

WOOD 1 (*raising hand woodenly and freezing*): Hola, Hello.

WOOD 2 (*raising hand woodenly and freezing*): Hola, Hello.

STORYTELLER 3: They stared ahead woodenly. They understood nothing.

(SOUND CREW 5 *strikes wood block as* WOOD PEOPLE *point index finger to head, opening eyes wide to show that they know nothing.*)

STORYTELLER 4: Their cheeks sucked in hollow.

(SOUND CREW 5 *strikes wood block as* WOOD PEOPLE *suck in cheeks.*)

STORYTELLER 1: They were taught to praise the gods, but they shook their heads, shrugged their shoulders, and forgot.

(SOUND CREW 5 *strikes wood block as* WOOD PEOPLE *shake heads, shrug shoulders, and stare blankly forward.*)

STORYTELLER 2: The Sun God and Moon Goddess made angry gestures. These people were heartless and ungrateful.

(SOUND CREW 6 *strikes low, rumbling piano notes as the actors gesture angrily.*)

STORYTELLER 3: They sent jagged, pitch black rain to destroy the Wood People.

(SOUND CREW 1 *strikes bass drum rapidly.* SOUND CREW 1–5 *shake rattles.* SOUND CREW 3 *shakes tambourine as each* RAIN *actor takes one area of stage and swirls angrily up, down, and all around* WOOD PEOPLE. *Take time to create the effect. Finally,* SOUND CREW 3 *slaps tambourine emphatically in center and* RAIN *freezes in jagged positions.* RAIN *sits.*)

STORYTELLER 4: But the rain did not destroy them. The Wood People climbed a ceiba tree.

(SOUND CREW 5 *strikes wood block as* CEIBA TREE *forms center;* WOOD PEOPLE *stoop low, then slowly stand and mime climbing the tree.*)

STORYTELLER 1: But the tree shook them off.

(SOUND CREW 1–5 *shake rattles vigorously.* SOUND CREW 1 *strikes drum once emphatically as* WOOD PEOPLE *fall off* CEIBA TREE.)

STORYTELLER 2: They crawled into a cave.

(SOUND CREW 3 *scrapes guiro to show the effort as* WOOD PEOPLE *crawl in slow motion to* CAVE *and go in.*)

STORYTELLER 3: But the cave heaved them out.

(SOUND CREW 3 *shakes tambourine for the heaving and slaps it once emphatically as* WOOD PEOPLE *roll over and freeze.*)

STORYTELLER 4: Their dogs growled and bared their teeth.

(DOGS *raise paws, growling, freezing, and baring teeth.*)

STORYTELLER 1: The Wood People had never fed them.

DOG 1 (*growling and pointing*): You never fed me.

DOG 2 (*barking and raising paw*): You never played with me.

STORYTELLER 2: The Wood People stared woodenly.

STORYTELLER 3: Their kitchen pots raised up. The Wood People had burned them when they cooked.

(DOGS *remain frozen.*)

POT 1 (*showing burned pot bottom and shaking it*): You burn, burn, burn me.

(SOUND CREW 4 *strikes gong.* POT *freezes.*)

POT 2 (*showing burned pot bottom and shaking it*): You burn, burn, burn me, too.

(SOUND CREW 4 *strikes gong.* POTS *freeze.*)

STORYTELLER 4: The stone used for grinding corn howled that the Wood People ground her down.

GRINDING STONE (*holding up pestle and twisting it as if grinding*): You grind, grind, grind my face.

(SOUND CREW 3 *scrapes guiro three times.* GRINDING STONE *freezes.*)

STORYTELLER 1: They all raised up high against the Wood People.

(*All lean forward, holding props high and glaring.*)

STORYTELLER 2: The dogs barked.

DOG (*raising paws higher*): Bark, bark, bark.

STORYTELLER 3: The pots cried, "Burn."

POT (*raising pot higher*): Burn, burn, burn.

(SOUND CREW 4 *strikes gong three times.*)

STORYTELLER 4: The grinding stone howled, "Grind."

GRINDING STONE (*raising pestle highest of all the props*): Grind, grind, grind.

(SOUND CREW 3 *scrapes guiro three times.*)

STORYTELLER 1: The Wood People put their hands to their ears and ran like monkeys into the forest.

(WOOD PEOPLE *pick up stump cloths and run to their chairs, bent over and arms out like monkeys.* SOUND CREW 5 *strikes wood block for running. Before sitting,* WOOD PEOPLE *face audience, freezing.*)

Developing Scripts for Myths and Tales

STORYTELLER 2 (*pointing to* WOOD PEOPLE): The descendants of those Wood People are monkeys.

(WOOD PEOPLE *step forward and glare like monkeys at audience.*)

STORYTELLER 3: That is why monkeys look like people.

(WOOD PEOPLE *glare at audience and then sit like monkeys.*)

Scene Four

Characters   Storytellers, Moon Goddess, Sun God, Corn People, Magic Grandmother, Mist

STORYTELLER 4: The Sun God and Moon Goddess stepped toward each other, down-hearted.

(SOUND CREW 6 *strikes two low piano notes as* SUN GOD *and* MOON GODDESS *step to center, facing audience and looking down.*)

STORYTELLER 1: They wanted people to praise them. They wanted people there with them at the first dawn. And dawn would come soon.

STORYTELLER 2: Suddenly they saw four ears of corn.

(*Four* CORN PEOPLE, *each holding an ear of corn, walk downstage.* SOUND CREW 2 *dings triangle as each of the* CORN PEOPLE *places its ear of corn on the floor and kneels behind it with head hidden.*)

STORYTELLER 3: Magic Grandmother picked up each ear of corn.

(SOUND CREW 2 *dings triangle as* GRANDMOTHER *picks up each ear.*)

STORYTELLER 4: She placed them in a circle.

(GRANDMOTHER *places corn stage center, kneeling behind it.*)

STORYTELLER 1: First she ground the ears into drinks.

(SOUND CREW 3 *scrapes guiro as* GRANDMOTHER *mimes grinding.*)

STORYTELLER 2: She fed drinks to the ears of corn.

(SOUND CREW 2 *rings bell as* GRANDMOTHER *stands and pours drink over* CORN PEOPLE.)

STORYTELLER 3: The ears of corn knelt, becoming Corn People with muscles of power.

(SOUND CREW 2 *dings triangle as* CORN PEOPLE *kneel, displaying strong muscles.*)

STORYTELLER 4: Magic Grandmother kneaded corn dough into flesh. The Corn People examined the flesh in wonder.

(SOUND CREW 5 *scrapes sand blocks as* GRANDMOTHER *kneads.* SOUND CREW 2 *dings triangle as* CORN PEOPLE *stretch out hands and arms, examining their flesh in wonder.*)

STORYTELLER 1: She placed two cobs near each of their corn bodies to form legs.

(GRANDMOTHER *picks up two ears of corn and stands by each* CORN PERSON, *miming placing two legs on each. Each stands, first kneeling on one leg and then standing on both when second is placed.* SOUND CREW 5 *strikes wood block as each leg forms.*)

STORYTELLER 2: The Corn People stood firmly.

STORYTELLER 3: Two cobs were placed for arms.

(GRANDMOTHER *stands behind each* CORN PERSON *and mimes placing the two other ears as arms.* SOUND CREW 5 *strikes wood block as she places each arm.*)

STORYTELLER 4: The Corn People spread their arms and opened them out gracefully into the world.

(CORN PEOPLE *reach out arms in graceful, flowing gesture as each arm is placed.*)

STORYTELLER 1: The Corn People looked high into the heart of the sky.

STORYTELLER 2: They looked deep into the heart of earth.

STORYTELLER 3: They bowed, saying "Gracias" to the creators for their life.

CORN 1 (*bowing to gods, reverently*): Gracias.

CORN 2 (*bowing to gods, reverently*): Gracias.

CORN 3 (*bowing to gods, reverently*): Gracias.

CORN 4 (*bowing deepest and most reverently*): Muchas gracias.

STORYTELLER 4: They felt godlike as they looked again high into the heart of the sky.

(SOUND CREW 2 *dings triangle as* CORN PEOPLE *open arms wide and look up.*)

STORYTELLER 1: And deep into the heart of Earth.

(SOUND CREW 2 *dings triangle as* CORN PEOPLE *extend arms down and look down deep.*)

STORYTELLER 2: But the gods were not happy. They shook their heads, crossed their arms, and stared forward.

STORYTELLER 3: These people knew too much.

STORYTELLER 4: Soon people might think they are gods.

MOON GODDESS: We made a mistake.

SUN GOD (*nodding*): Yes, we made a big mistake.

STORYTELLER 1: They conferred.

(*The two come together at center stage and whisper.*)

STORYTELLER 2: They leaned forward, and with their whole face and body, they blew a great mist into the Corn People's eyes.

(SOUND CREW 1–5 *shake rattles for blowing.*)

STORYTELLER 3: The Corn People squinted.

STORYTELLER 4: They tried to push the mist away with their hands.

STORYTELLER 1: But they could not. And from that day to this, people can see only so far. They cannot see as much as the gods.

STORYTELLER 2: They squint trying to see high into the heart of the sky and squint trying to look deep into the heart of the earth.

Scene Five

Characters Storytellers, Moon Goddess, Sun God, Corn People, Dawn, Golden Light, Sun, Lake, Palm Tree, Rock, Thunder Gods, Corn God

STORYTELLER 3: It was almost time for the first dawn.

STORYTELLER 4: The people turned toward the east.

(CORN PEOPLE *and* GODS *turn their backs to audience, looking toward rear of stage for* DAWN.)

STORYTELLER 1: They waited patiently.

STORYTELLER 2: They waited and waited and waited and thought the dawn would never come.

STORYTELLER 3: Suddenly an orange light shimmered.

(SOUND CREW 6 *sweeps glissando on high piano notes as* DAWN *actors quickly form upstage and shimmer orange netting.*)

STORYTELLER 4: There was a golden gleaming.

(SOUND CREW 3 *shakes tambourine and wind chimes as* GOLDEN LIGHT *shimmers behind cloth.*)

STORYTELLER 1: The sun slowly rose and spread its beams.

(SOUND CREW 2 *strikes triangle five times as* SUN *kneels, hiding head; on a slow count of five, actor grows into sun with rays outstretched.* DAWN *returns to seat, trailing dawn cloth and inconspicuously dropping it behind chairs.*)

STORYTELLER 2: The lake sparkled with happiness.

(SOUND CREW 2 *rings bells and* SOUND CREW 3 *rings wind chimes as* LAKE *forms and shimmers lightly.*)

STORYTELLER 3: The palm tree swayed.

(PALM TREE *stands and sways.* SOUND CREW 2 *rings bells and* SOUND CREW 3 *rings wind chimes as* PALM TREE *sways.*)

STORYTELLER 4: Birds sang.

(SOUND CREW 2 *rings bells. All actors make bird whistles.*)

STORYTELLER 1: The Corn People knelt and bowed in thanks.

(CORN PEOPLE *kneel and bow heads.*)

The Creation and the Birth of the Corn God

STORYTELLER 2: Suddenly all was silent.

(SOUND CREW 2 *dings triangle as everyone freezes.*)

STORYTELLER 3: Something new was about to emerge.

STORYTELLER 4: They saw a rock.

(ROCK *stands and moves to center, upstage of* CORN PEOPLE, *holding cloth up straight and rigid to conceal* CORN GOD, *who goes behind it.* CORN GOD *carries costume concealed and puts it on behind rock.*)

STORYTELLER 1: Something was under the rock.

STORYTELLER 2: The people pushed the rock with all their might.

(CORN PEOPLE, *staying a few feet in front of* ROCK, *mime pushing the* ROCK *with exertion.*)

STORYTELLER 3: It would not budge.

STORYTELLER 4: Thunder gods hurled thunder bolts at it.

(SOUND CREW 1 *strikes drums staccato and then strikes drum once emphatically as* THUNDER GODS *stand and mime hurling bolts all over the* ROCK. THUNDER GODS *freeze and sit.*)

STORYTELLER 1: The rock cracked.

(SOUND CREW 1 *plays bass drum staccato,* ROCK *moves cloth as if slowly cracking. Only one* ROCK *actor lets the cloth drop. The other holds up half of the cloth.*)

STORYTELLER 2: A youth emerged in a headdress of gold and green. The youth looked down and held out an ear of corn. The youth was their Corn God.

(CORN GOD *steps majestically center holding one hand up in welcoming gesture and bestowing on them the gift of corn with the other.*)

STORYTELLER 3: These people had come from corn.

STORYTELLER 4: Now they had a Corn God to worship.

STORYTELLER 1: They bowed and raised up their ears of corn.

(CORN PEOPLE *kneel and stretch arms out, holding up ears of corn.*)

STORYTELLER 2: And then they did a dance to honor the Corn God.

STORYTELLER 3: We do one now for you today.

(SOUND CREW 1 *plays taped music, and the dancers do the same dance as at the beginning of the play, except this time the* CORN PEOPLE *raise and lower ears of corn as they dance, and the* CORN GOD *stands in the center as they all circle in worship. When music fades, dancers move, following the circle, to their chairs. Music does not fully fade until the last dancer sits. Then* STORYTELLER 1 *moves to stage center for the finale.*)

The Creation and the Birth of the Corn God

Finale

STORYTELLER 1: Gracias students, adults, too.

STORYTELLER 2: For watching so kindly our show for you.

STORYTELLER 3: Of a Mayan myth, old yet new.

STORYTELLER 4: We hope it came alive for you.

STORYTELLER 1: And here's a last tip from us, your friends.

STORYTELLER 2 (*holding up a book of Mayan myths or culture*): Read a book of these myths from beginning to end.

STORYTELLER 3: And study different cultures wherever they may be.

STORYTELLER 4: For the more that you know, the more you'll be...

(STORYTELLERS *gesture to all performers.*)

EVERYONE (*making big circular gesture around their heads*): Free!

STORYTELLER 1: The actors are...

STORYTELLER 2: The Sound Crew is...

STORYTELLER 3: The Storytellers are...

STORYTELLER 4: Gracias.

To end the performance, STORYTELLERS 1–4 introduce the performers, having them stand and say their names loudly and clearly. When all are standing, STORYTELLERS 1–4 turn toward them and raise arms. Everyone follows, raising their arms and bringing them down together for a group bow, saying "Gracias" as they do so. Performers then sit for the audience performance discussion.

Story Questions and Research Topics

To spark students' interest and enrich the cultural experience, provide a variety of materials for investigation, dramatic play, study, and observation. Suggestions include artifacts, clothing, utensils, photographs, artwork, and books. Discussion questions and research topics can be pursued before embarking on a drama experience, during play rehearsal, or after the production to support the culture being introduced.

Story Questions

1. How do you know the Moon Goddess and the Sun God were powerful?
2. Why are people in this myth expected to be respectful to the Sun God and Moon Goddess? What happens when they aren't?
3. What was wrong with the Mud People?
4. What was wrong with the Wood People?
5. Why did the gods approve of the Corn People?
6. Why didn't the gods create people from corn in the first place?
7. What else might the gods have used to create people?
8. Why do you think the Mayans believed people came from corn?
9. What is the climax, or the most exciting moment, in this story?
10. What is the tone of this story—serious, funny, magical, or a combination of these? Explain.
11. What is your favorite scene in this story? Why?
12. What characters do you like best? Why?

Theater-Performance Questions

1. The Mayans and other cultures made their musical instruments with *local* materials, materials found near where they lived. Instruments included drums, whistles, flutes, jingles, and rattles. What kind of instruments might you create with objects found around your home or school? Describe how you might make an instrument. Create your own instrument, decorate it, and use it for the dance in this play.

2. Ancient accounts of the Mayans and other cultures mention that people danced and sang to honor their gods and to ask for help. How might music and dancing have influenced or impressed the gods?

Research Topics

1. In ancient Mayan and other early cultures, the gods were thought to help people, but they expected payment and often wanted it in advance. Why do you think the gods wanted payment in advance? How did the Mayans pay the Corn God in advance?

2. The Corn God was considered to be the central god of all vegetation even though the Mayans had other plant gods, such as a god of squash. Why do you think the Corn God was the central one?

3. The Mayans worshiped corn, and even today some people in Central America call it "your grace." Why is corn so important to them? Why might we take such things for granted?

4. The Corn God or Maize God, as he is often called, always appears as a young man about fifteen or sixteen years old. Why do you think he is depicted as a youth?

5. Many believe civilization in the New World occurred when people learned to grow corn. What does creating a civilization mean? At first, people had to move around to hunt animals for food to live. When they grew corn, they could live in one place. How would living in one place help a society and civilization form?

6. The Mayans made beautiful objects out of feathers. Priests often wore fabulous headdresses of feathers in religious ceremonies. What might be the symbolism of the feathers?

7. In the 1500s, missionaries from Spain came to the Yucatan and other areas where the Mayans lived. Some wrote down the stories and history of the Mayans that Mayans told to them. One friar, Diego del Landa, recorded stories about the gods and their deeds that told the history of the people. What is the value today of knowing these myths?

8. Corn was essential to the Mayans. What are some of the food products that come from corn? What can be made from corn that is not food? What is your favorite way to eat corn? In what way is corn especially important in the diet of most people in Central America?

9. The Corn God is often shown with long hair. Why is his hair long and not short? What part of corn might his long hair represent?

10. The Mayans are described as being devout, moderate, and disciplined. These qualities are probably shared by the makers of other great cultures. How might these traits help a people form a great civilization?

11. The formation of a great civilization requires a few creative people with a lot of imagination and mental energy. What does this mean? Why are these needed to get a great civilization started and to keep it going?

12. When the Mayans discovered how to grow corn, they worked hard to cultivate their crops during the summer, but were able to take time off from October until spring. Thus, they had leisure time. How might having leisure time help people build a civilization?

13. Central designs on Mayan sculpture are the serpent, the feathers of the quetzal bird, and leaves of the corn plant. Find out why these designs were chosen. Collect pictures illustrating these designs.

14. The ancient Mayan civilization is called *Pre-Colombian*. What does Pre-Colombian mean? Why is the history of the area divided this way?

15. Many books have been written about the ancient Mayan civilization, which was considered to be creative and great in many ways. Collect pictures depicting the powerful Mayan art and describe some of the great Mayan achievements.

16. The Mayans lived in the Yucatan, Chiapas, Guatemala, and parts of Honduras and El Salvador. Find these locations on a map. People marvel at the ability of the Mayan people to grow corn in these regions. Study the terrain and explain why this was an amazing feat.

17. Find out some of the reasons given for the decline of the Mayan civilization. When did it happen? When did the culture flourish?

18. The Mayans left more of a record of their stories and history than any other early Native American group. They did not have writing as we know it. Find out how they left records of their stories and lives.

19. Some cultures have a goddess of vegetation, grain, or corn rather than a god. Find a story or culture that honors a goddess in this way. Find or draw a picture and tell or write a story about her.

20. The Sun God and Moon Goddess were two of the most important Mayan gods. What other cultures consider these gods to be important? Research other cultures represented in this book to learn about other significant gods.

21. The Mayan myth shows the gods trying two times to create people before they made the Corn People they liked. The Aztecs, another Hispanic culture, believed the same thing. Read an Aztec creation myth showing how people were formed. How is it similar? How is it different?

22. Not all early cultures believed people were created from corn. Study another early culture and find out where it thought the first people came from.

23. The Mayans believe in *animism,* that everything in nature has a soul. They believe that rocks and plants could help or hurt them in their endeavors. What other cultures represented in this book believe all nature has these kinds of powers?

Selected Bibliography
Hispanic Stories and Poems

Bierhorst, John. *Doctor Coyote: A Native American Aesop's Fables*. Illustrated by Wendy Watson. New York: Macmillan, Inc., 1987. Delightful versions of twenty of Aesop's fables as they were retold by the Aztecs in the 1500s.

———, ed. *The Monkey's Haircut and Other Stories Told by the Maya*. Illustrated by Robert Andrew Parker. New York: William Morrow and Company, 1986. Myths, trickster tales, and other stories dating back to the time of the ancient Mayans for ages nine and above.

Brenner, Anita. *The Boy Who Could Do Anything and Other Mexican Folk Tales*. Illustrated by Jean Charlot. Hamden, CT: Linnet Books, 1992. Reissue of twenty-six short, authentic folk tales. Some are good to dramatize.

dePaola, Tomie. *The Lady of Guadalupe*. New York: Holiday House, 1980. Vivid illustrations depict the story of Mexico's patron saint. Also published in a Spanish language version.

Kouzel, Daisy. *The Cuckoo's Reward/El Premio del Cuco*. Illustrated by Earl Thollander. New York: Doubleday, 1977. Written in both English and Spanish, this adaptation of a Mayan myth is excellent to dramatize.

Lattimore, Deborah Nourse. *Why There Is No Arguing in Heaven: A Mayan Myth*. New York: Harper and Row, 1989. Excellent illustrations accompany the creation myth adapted in this book. This version is similar to the play version used here, making it an excellent choice for comparing and contrasting.

Martinez, Alejandro Cruz. *The Woman Who Outshone the Sun*. Illustrated by Fernando Olivers. Emeryville, CA: Children's Book Press, 1991. This Zapotec legend of a beautiful woman who takes away the river from the villagers who scorn her is told in both English and Spanish.

Richard, Lewis. *All of You Was Singing*. Illustrated by Ed Young. New York: Atheneum, 1991. Aztec myth telling of Earth's creation and the origin of music.

Rohmer, Harriet, and Mary Anchondo. *How We Came to the Fifth World/Como Vinimos al Quinto Mundo: A Creation Story from Ancient Mexico*. Emeryville, CA: Children's Book Press, 1988. Bright, bold, primitive illustrations complement this bilingual Aztec tale of the creation and destruction of the world by Aztec gods.

Schon, Isabel, ed. *Dona Blanca and Other Hispanic Nursery Rhymes and Games*. Minneapolis: T. S. Denison, 1983. Bilingual publication of eighteen Mexican rhymes and games, with instructions on how to play them.

Wisniewski, David. *Rain Player*. New York: Clarion Books, 1991. Ancient Mayan tale of a ball player who challenges the rain god to a game in order to end the drought.

Cultural Information

Blackmore, Vivien. *Why Corn is Golden: Stories About Plants.* Illustrated by Susana Martinez-Ostos. Boston: Little Brown and Company, 1984. Six Pre-Columbian legends and riddles beautifully illustrated with images of flowers, fruits, and plants.

McKissack, Patricia. *The Maya.* Emeryville, CA: Children's Book Press, 1985. Easy-to-read text and excellent photos show the history, religion, and customs of the Mayans.

Neurath, Marie. *They Lived Like This: The Ancient Maya.* Illustrated by John Ellis. New York: Franklin Watts, 1966. Authentic drawings based on Mayan wall paintings and designs describe outstanding aspects of Mayan civilization: pottery, agriculture, gods, cities, religious buildings, pyramids, jewelry, ceremonies, wars, houses, astronomy, the calendar, and mathematics.

Politi, Leo. *Three Stalks of Corn.* New York: Charles Scribner's Sons, 1976. Reissue of a charming picture book in which Angelica's grandmother tells of legends about corn and shows its many uses today.

Trout, Lawana Hooper. *The Maya.* New York: Chelsea House Publications, 1991. Informative and comprehensive. Excellent for student reports showing the development of Mayan civilization and the Mayans today.

CHAPTER SEVEN

Coyote and the Swallowing Monster
A Nez Percé Transformation Myth

Coyote is one of the most frequent symbols in Native American mythology. He is the best known of the trickster figures, and is celebrated as a hero and creator. This story stakes place in the Transformation Age, when the world was coming into being. Coyote helps to transform the world for the human race.

As the world was waiting patiently for human beings to arrive, Coyote sensed that something was wrong: the Monster had swallowed all of The People! Following his nose and the advice of Aunt Meadowlark, Coyote passed through a lake where he washed himself, and came upon the huge Monster. With a force that swept up all the underground seeds and spread them across the earth, Monster inhaled deeply, capturing Coyote in his mouth. Clever Coyote traveled down Monster's throat, past Grizzly Bear, Rattlesnake, and helpful Brown Bear, to the place where The People were trapped inside. Using his ingenuity, Coyote helped The People build a fire inside Monster's stomach. The fire and smoke made Monster sick, but it did not kill him or free The People. So Coyote used a stone knife to cut away at Monster's heart. Monster's heart was so strong that the knife broke. The same thing happened for a second knife, and then a third, fourth, and fifth knife. Finally Monster died, and Coyote beckoned all those who were captured inside Monster to escape through Monster's mouth. A lone Muskrat was the last to escape. Coyote used sharp knives to carve up Monster's body into portions, and he distributed these portions throughout the world. By doing so, he showed where each tribe of People would live and explained why Coyote is a favorite hero of the Nez Percé.

Acting Exercises

The following acting exercises may be used to help students practice acting principles and develop the characters that make up the cast of this play.

Becoming Coyote

Goal   To experience Coyote's basic stance and actions.

Acting Principles   Belief, Control.

Procedure   Divide the class into two groups. Have each group act out every other Coyote scene described below and then create a frozen picture of it. Have groups comment on each other's believable, controlled acting.

- Peer out from your den. Sniff the air for enemies. Trot like a coyote (built like a person) on two feet. Freeze.
- Trot in place. Discover twigs. Weave a sturdy trap to catch salmon. Freeze. Hear something. Sniff and scan the horizon. Examine your work. Freeze.
- Trot to the Monster, up high ridges and down low ones, up and down, up and down. Freeze. See a lake. Dive in and swim to clean off. Roll in place in clay to camouflage yourself. Examine your coat. Freeze.
- Trot. Discover five stone flint knives. Pick up each one. Test their sharpness. Test their hardness. Put each in your backpack. Howl three times with pleasure. Freeze.
- Trot alertly, sniffing and peering for Monster. Freeze, sensing something. See Monster's huge eyeball. Show your reaction. Freeze.
- Crouch behind a bush. Examine Monster. Consider how to trick him. Freeze. Gather your courage. Stand tall. Call confidently, "Monster! Oh Monster! You swallow me." Freeze.
- Position yourself, ready for Monster to inhale you. Feel yourself being yanked up from the ground like a tornado. Spin three times into Monster's mouth. Freeze, showing how you feel.
- Trot to Monster's heart. Brown Bear looms, but you loom stronger. Freeze.
- Show your determination to destroy the evil heart of Monster. Say, "I *must* destroy the evil heart." Pick up each of the five knives and cut. Cut harder each time. Toss each knife away when it breaks. Yank the one remaining heart thread with both hands. Exert force. Show your success. Freeze.

Becoming Parts of Monster

Goal   To mime Monster's body parts.

Acting Principles   Belief, Control.

Procedure   Again divide the class into two groups. This time let both groups act out all of the scenes described below, using believable, controlled acting.

- Become Monster's huge, peering eyeball. Roll around looking for Coyote. Freeze.
- Become Monster's huge sniffing nostril. Sniff all around for Coyote. Freeze.
- Become (in pairs) a huge open mouth. Chew up a few pine trees. Freeze.
- Use your whole body to become the Monster's heart, thumping. Freeze.

Becoming Minor Characters and Objects

Goal   To mime the actions of various characters and depict inanimate objects.

Acting Principles   Belief, Voice and Movement.

Procedure   Divide the class into two groups; each group acts out every other one of the following actions, characters, or objects in the story.

- Pile up wood. Light a fire. Become the fire, warming people.
- Fly lightly as Aunt Meadowlark. Land. Feel Coyote stepping on your delicate foot. Show your reaction. Freeze.
- Become Grizzly Bear, raising vicious claws over Coyote. Freeze. Coyote looms at you. Show your reaction. Hit your nose on a ledge. Growl and show your reaction. Freeze.
- In pairs or singly, become the jagged ledge Grizzly hits his nose on.
- Become Rattlesnake. Hiss and slither at Coyote. Freeze. Coyote hisses at you. Show your reaction. Hit your head on a ledge. Hiss. Freeze.
- Become the whirling Smoke, trying to make Monster cough up the people. Freeze.
- Become in rapid succession powerful Buffalo, innocent Mouse, enormous Bear, soaring Eagle. Freeze after each character is named.

Becoming the Monster Chorus

Goal   To coordinate sound effects with action.

Acting Principle   Voice and Movement.

Procedure   Assign four students to the role of Storytellers, while the rest of the class becomes the chorus. Ask the Storytellers to give the cues described below and have students (most of whom will become Monster) respond as the Monster Chorus. If desired, the Sound Crew can make the sound effect given in the script for each response.

- Storyteller cue: The mouth laughed.

  Monster Chorus (mouths open wide and rocking body back and forth rhythmically): Ha, ha, ha. You swallow me first.

- Storyteller cue: Monster's turn. He inhaled one, two, three.

  Chorus (deeply inhaling): One, two, three.

- Storyteller cue: The heart thumped.

  Chorus (moving rhythmically): Thump, thump, thump.

- Storyteller cue: Monster's mouth coughed.

  Chorus: Cough, cough, cough.

- Storyteller cue: Nostrils wiggled furiously and sneezed.

  Chorus: Achoo, achoo, achoo.

- Storyteller cue: Eyeballs teared.

  Chorus: Boo, hoo, hoo.

- Storyteller cue: Monster yelled "Stop."

  Chorus: Stop.

- Storyteller cue: The smoke made Monster sick. He fainted.

  Chorus (in slow motion, swooning, ending on sides): Oooooh.

- Storyteller cue: Monster groaned and writhed in agony.

  Chorus (writhing in slow motion): Ohhhhh.

- Storyteller cue: Monster fell over dead.

  Chorus (emphatically): Dead.

Slow-Motion Pulling and Falling

Goal To act a vigorous part of the play with control.

Acting Principle Control.

Procedure This activity need only be done by the four People and Muskrat who enact it in the play. It is helpful for others to learn control techniques through observation. The four People must pretend to pull out Muskrat from inside Monster's nostrils and then fall down when he pops out.

To do this with control, the People stand on one side and pretend to pull Muskrat in slow motion, showing great exertion. When Muskrat pops out, the People fall onto the floor in slow motion in one direction and Muskrat falls in the other direction.

Exerting Nature's Power

Goal To develop the imagination and experience a Native North American Indian belief.

Acting Principles Belief, Voice and Movement.

Procedure Explain that some Native North American Indian groups believe that everything in nature has its own magnetic power or *orenda*, as the Iroquois call it. For example, a snake thrusting its head forward is exerting its orenda. Everything tries to effect its influence in the world by exerting its orenda.

Have the whole class create frozen pictures showing the power or orenda of Coyote, Swirling Snow, Lake, Grizzly Bear, Rattlesnake, Monster's Heart, Smoke, and Eagle. Have students suggest other characters and objects to portray.

Production Notes

The following guidelines may be used to enhance the quality of the production with dance movements and simple costumes.

Eagle Power Dance

Music   "The Rabbit Dance," from the audio tape entitled *Songs of Earth, Water, Fire and Sky*. Available from New World Records, 701 Seventh Avenue, New York, NY, 10036, or from Rounder Round Up, 1-800-443-4727, which offers authentic Native American music of several regions. Students might also do this dance using only a steady drum beat and rattles.

Purpose and Style   To honor the eagle. Perhaps explain that "Eagle Power" is desired by all Native North American Indians. Discuss what is meant by Eagle Power. How might knowing the purpose help a person do this dance? The dance is controlled and focused; the aim of the dancer is to climb into the spirit and soul of the eagle in order to identify with it.

Materials   Students might wear decorative headdresses. Gourd players might make their own rattles from containers decorated with bold designs and filled with pop-corn. Leader carries feather dusters in earth tones to represent wings.

Formation   A circle moving clockwise.

Steps and Stances   The basic step is the Tap step. First tap the ball of the left foot, and then step down on the foot. Repeat on the right foot. Continue doing this. Students might do the Tap step in time to a drum. Arms move up and down to resemble an eagle flapping its wings. Head nods gently in various directions to resemble an eagle's head movements.

> *Step One:* Lead dancer stands upstage center holding feather dusters out to sides representing wings. Two gourd players with rattles stand on either side of leader. As the music begins, the gourd players shake their rattles. The Sound Crew lightly plays bells, drum, or rattles to blend in. Leader does Tap step, flapping wings to down center.

Tap Step

> *Step Two:* Reaching down center, leader stops and circles in place twice, doing the Tap step and flapping.

> *Step Three:* Leader stops, faces performers, and raises wings, signaling all to stand.

Step Four: Leader checks to see that all are ready. Leader turns clockwise, signaling performers to turn, too. All circle the stage twice, Tap-stepping, nodding, and flapping.

Step Five: After circling twice, leader stops downstage center (at same point where group began), raises one wing and keeps the other down by side, and circles in place to the right. All performers do this step and then repeat it in the opposite direction.

Step Five

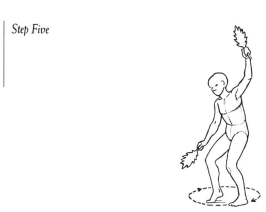

Step Six (Optional): Remaining in place, all dancers flap wings as they stoop and come up.

Step Six

Leader turns clockwise. Performers follow and all Tap step to their chairs. Music fades when last performer sits. Performers quickly put on costumes. Storyteller One begins the first lines of the play, speaking in an enthusiastic voice to grab the audience's attention.

Finale The final dance at the conclusion of the play is the same as the opening dance, except that Coyote dances the role of the leader and stands in the center of the circle of dancers.

Costume Suggestions

For narrative mime presentations, all students wear black clothing—black shirts and black pants—with individual character costumes worn as additional pieces to the all-black attire.

Storytellers   Beaded or otherwise decorative headbands, with feathers attached. Fringed tunics of "suede cloth," if available, to resemble deerskin; use brown cloth if suede cloth is not available.

Developing Scripts for Myths and Tales

Coyote   Brown baseball cap adapted with tall coyote ears made from stiff tag board painted brown or covered with fabric; feathers can be loosely attached to the cap so that they bounce when he trots. Breach cloth (similar to an apron with panels of cloth in front and back made of appropriate Native American Indian-style fabric). Beige or off-white leg warmers worn with matching shoes make good leggings. Coyote's staff can be made from a one-inch thick dowel about two feet long, decorated with colorful yarn, fake eagle feathers, and strips of fake fur.

The People   Matching headbands, either plain or of an appropriate design, with a feather stuck in the side.

Swirling Snow   White strips of crepe paper, white ribbons, or fabric cut into strips (about one yard long) and taped to a dowel. Two for each Snow actor.

Gold Fire   Gold tinsel or ribbons several inches long attached to a dowel or made into a pompon.

Aunt Meadowlark   Black, white, or gray baseball cap with black fabric or drawn spots on it.

Lake   Aqua-colored fabric, about two yards square.

Monster's Eyes   Black wool caps or the tops of two pairs of black panty hose, cut off and worn on the head (but not over the face unless an opening for the face is cut) to represent the eye's pupil. Arms held in a circle around the head create the eyeball.

Monster's Nostrils   Arms are held in triangular shape and moved back and forth and side to side to represent breathing.

Monster's Mouth   Red turtleneck shirt and red gloves. The two actors create a big, round, open mouth with their arms and hands.

Monster's Body   Students sit with legs crossed in a circle.

Boys   Matching headbands and feathers (different colors than those of The People).

Grizzly Bear   Black furry hat.

Ledges for Grizzly Bear and Rattlesnake   Created by actors' bodies.

Brown Bear   Brown furry hat, possibly with ears attached.

Monster's Heart   Red umbrella with large heart drawn on it. Heart is outlined with a three-inch border of black felt-tipped pen or black shoe polish. The actor opens and closes the umbrella to represent heart thumping and beating.

Monster's Heart Thread   Red ribbon tied to the umbrella's fastener and held taut.

Red Fire   Red tinsel or ribbons several inches long attached to a dowel or made into a pompon.

Smoke   Strips of black cloth, crepe paper, or ribbon, about one inch wide and one yard long, attached to a dowel.

Muskrat   Gray hat with small, pointy ears attached. Rope attached to pants for a tail.

Colors—White, Green, Black, and Gold   Banners of shiny material of each color, about thirty-six inches long and twelve inches wide, or pennants made of these materials and attached to sticks.

Buffalo   Brown furry hat with horns attached.

Mouse   Gray or brown baseball cap or other animal headpiece with small, pointy ears attached. Ears might be lined in pink.

Bear   Black baseball cap with ears attached.

Eagle   White baseball cap with yellow fabric covering the brim to represent a bill.

Fox   Orange baseball cap with small ears attached.

Coyote and
the Swallowing Monster
A Nez Percé Transformation Myth

Cast

FOUR STORYTELLERS (responsible, with strong, clear, enthusiastic voices and gestures)

COYOTE (lively, creative, uninhibited; a natural actor)

FOUR PEOPLE (loud voices, alert)

SWIRLING SNOW (3)

GOLD FIRE (2)

AUNT MEADOWLARK (lively)

LAKE (2)

MONSTER'S EYE (2)

MONSTER'S NOSTRILS (2)

MONSTER'S MOUTH (2)

BOY (2)

GRIZZLY BEAR

LEDGE FOR GRIZZLY BEAR (2)

RATTLESNAKE

LEDGE FOR RATTLESNAKE (2)

BROWN BEAR

MONSTER'S HEART (2)

MONSTER'S HEART THREAD

RED FIRE

SMOKE (3)

MUSKRAT

COLOR WHITE

BUFFALO

COLOR GREEN

MOUSE

COLOR BLACK

BEAR

COLOR GOLD

EAGLE

FOX

MONSTER'S BODY (played by all actors except Coyote; actors other than Monster's Eye, Nostrils, and Mouth also play characters in the body)

Adaptations For smaller groups, one student could portray Aunt Meadowlark, Snow, and Fire. The same students who might play both the Lake and the Ridges. In addition, you can limit the number of People to two instead of four.

◇ ▦◇▦◇▦ ◇ ▦◇▦◇▦ ◇ ▦◇▦◇▦ ◇ ▦◇▦◇▦ ◇ ▦◇▦◇▦ ◇ ▦◇▦◇▦ ◇ ▦◇▦◇▦ ◇ ▦◇▦◇▦ ◇

Sound Crew

SOUND CREW 1	taped music, wind chimes, rattle, guiro
SOUND CREW 2	wood block, wind chimes, rattle
SOUND CREW 3	tambourine, medium drum, rattle, sand blocks
SOUND CREW 4	triangle, bell, rattle
SOUND CREW 5	large drum, slide whistle, rattle, sand blocks
SOUND CREW 6	piano or resonator bells (does not need to know how to play piano), jingle bells, small drum

Basic Stage Setup

The actors sit on stage in chairs arranged in a semicircle in view of the audience. Costumes and props are stored under the actors' chairs and put on after the opening dance.

The Sound Crew sits with instruments on a table to the right of the stage area, in view of the audience. The tables are set so that the Crew can see the stage.

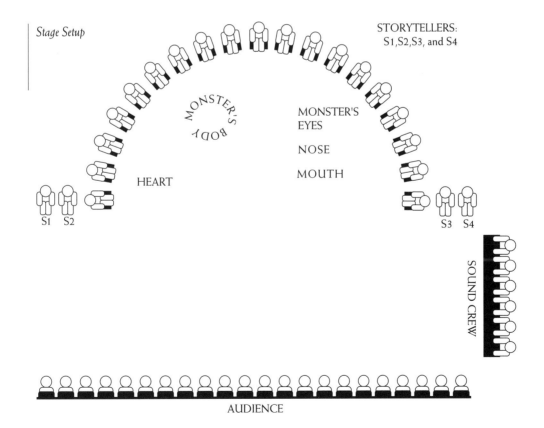

Stage Setup

STORYTELLERS: S1, S2, S3, and S4

MONSTER'S BODY

MONSTER'S EYES

NOSE

MOUTH

HEART

S1 S2

S3 S4

SOUND CREW

AUDIENCE

Copyright © Louise Thistle and Dale Seymour Publications

Coyote and the Swallowing Monster   115

SOUND CREW 1 *plays taped Native North American music and actors and* STORYTELLERS *per-form Eagle Power Dance. (See* Production Notes *for music and dance suggestions.)*

SOUND CREW *plays rattles, bells, and drums, blending in with but not overpowering the music. When the dance is over, the dancers dance to their places.* SOUND CREW 1 *fades music and* STORY-TELLER 1 *speaks in a bright, enthusiastic voice to catch the audience's attention.*

Scene One

Characters   Storytellers, People, Gold Fire, Coyote, Aunt Meadowlark

STORYTELLER 1: Imagine icy winter.

ALL ACTORS (*hugging themselves*): Brrrrr. Brrrrr.

STORYTELLER 2: Snow swirls outside.

(SOUND CREW 1 *and* SOUND CREW 2 *ring wind chimes as* SWIRLING SNOW *moves along front of stage, bending, whirling, and twisting; give time to create the effect.*)

STORYTELLER 3: We are huddled in the longhouse.

(*Actors hug themselves.*)

STORYTELLER 4: People pile up wood.

(SOUND CREW 2 *strikes wood block as the* FOUR PEOPLE *in turn stand, bend down, and mime carrying a heavy log to the hearth at center stage.* GOLD FIRE *takes place amidst logs of wood, hiding fire until it is lit.*)

STORYTELLER 1: Someone lights the fire.

(SOUND CREW 1 *scrapes guiro as* PEOPLE 1 *lights fire;* GOLD FIRE *leaps up.*)

STORYTELLER 2: The flames dance.

(SOUND CREW 3 *shakes tambourine lightly as* GOLD FIRE *dances.*)

STORYTELLER 3: Winter is story time.

(GOLD FIRE *returns to seat.*)

STORYTELLER 4 (*pointing first to actors and then to* STORYTELLERS): But first, if we tell the story, what will you give us?

PEOPLE 1 (*standing and opening hand*): Acorns?

ALL ACTORS (*vigorously shaking heads*): No.

PEOPLE 2: Pine cones?

ALL ACTORS (*vigorously shaking heads*): No.

PEOPLE 3: Beef jerky and huckleberries?

ALL ACTORS (*rubbing stomachs and nodding*): Hmmm. Okay.

STORYTELLER 1: The story of Coyote and the Swallowing Monster.

(SOUND CREW 4 *dings triangle.*)

STORYTELLER 2: The world was waiting for the human race.

(SOUND CREW 4 *dings triangle.*)

STORYTELLER 3: Coyote came trotting along.

(SOUND CREW 2 *taps wood block as* COYOTE *trots briskly, knees high.*)

STORYTELLER 4: He put together sticks crisscross and began building a fish ladder to trap salmon for People.

(SOUND CREW 2 *strikes wood block as* COYOTE *bends over, picks up twigs, and weaves them in and out.*)

STORYTELLER 1: Something called strongly to Coyote.

PEOPLE 1 (*standing, cupping hands; strongly*): What are you doing?

(SOUND CREW 4 *strikes triangle as* PEOPLE 1 *freezes with hands cupped.*)

PEOPLE 2 (*repeating* PEOPLE 1*'s action and expression*): What are you doing?

(SOUND CREW 4 *strikes triangle as* PEOPLE 2 *freezes, hands cupped.*)

STORYTELLER 2: Coyote looked.

(COYOTE *alertly scans stage left, right, up, and down.*)

STORYTELLER 3: Something declared, "The people are gone."

(COYOTE *tilts head to listen closely.*)

PEOPLE 3 (*standing, cupping hands; powerfully*): The people are gone.

(SOUND CREW 4 *strikes triangle.*)

PEOPLE 4 (*standing, cupping hands; powerfully*): The people are gone.

(SOUND CREW 4 *strikes triangle.*)

PEOPLE 1 (*most powerfully*): The Monster has swallowed them.

(SOUND CREW 3 *shakes tambourine vigorously and slaps the center for emphasis.*)

STORYTELLER 4: Coyote stopped.

COYOTE: I'd better stop what I'm doing. I'd better see about that monster.

STORYTELLER 1: Coyote trotted upstream.

(SOUND CREW 2 *taps wood block for trotting.*)

STORYTELLER 2: Aunt Meadowlark flew along.

(SOUND CREW 4 *rings bell for flying.* AUNT MEADOWLARK *sweeps about stage, arms open wide to represent wings.*)

STORYTELLER 3: Coyote stepped on Aunt Meadowlark's leg.

Developing Scripts for Myths and Tales

(As COYOTE trots *along, he and* AUNT MEADOWLARK *pass each other and he mimes stepping on* AUNT MEADOWLARK's *leg.* SOUND CREW 4 *dings triangle.*)

AUNT MEADOWLARK (*hopping up and down*): Luma, luma, luma. Ow, ow, ow.

COYOTE (*bowing*): I'm sorry. I was in a hurry to save the People from the Monster.

AUNT MEADOWLARK (*pointing first in one direction and then the other*): You won't find the Monster that way. He's this way.

COYOTE (*pointing*): I better go this way, too. Thank you.

Scene Two

Characters   Storytellers, Coyote, Lake

STORYTELLER 4: Coyote came to a shimmering lake, and decided to take a bath.

(SOUND CREW 1 *and* SOUND CREW 2 *ring wind chimes and* SOUND CREW 4 *rings bells as* LAKE *forms center and shimmers; take time for this effect.*)

COYOTE (*to audience, pointing to* LAKE): I'll take a bath to clean up. If I don't taste good, the Monster might spit me out.

STORYTELLER 1: Coyote dove in and swam back and forth five times.

(SOUND CREW 2 *strikes wood block as* LAKE *holds up cloth and* COYOTE *dives under it.* SOUND CREW 4 *and* SOUND CREW 6 *ring bells lightly as* COYOTE *swims; take time to create this effect.*)

STORYTELLER 2: Coyote covered himself with clay to blend with the scenery.

(SOUND CREW 3 *shakes tambourine as* COYOTE *steps out of water and rolls all over stage, covering himself with clay; use as much of the stage as possible.*)

STORYTELLER 3: He filled a backpack with five stone knives.

COYOTE (*picking knives up from all over stage*): One, two, three, four, five.

(SOUND CREW 2 *strikes wood block as* COYOTE *counts each knife.*)

STORYTELLER 4: Coyote felt equipped. He howled.

COYOTE (*throwing head way back and howling loudly, facing stage right, left, and finally center*): HOWWWL, HOWWWL, HOWWWL.

STORYTELLER 1: It was a long way to the monster.

STORYTELLER 2: Up ridges...

(SOUND CREW 6 *strikes piano notes from low to high;* COYOTE *raises up on tip toes for high.*)

STORYTELLER 3: And down.

(SOUND CREW 6 *strikes piano notes from high to low;* COYOTE *bends low.*)

STORYTELLER 4: Up...

(*Repeat sound and movement.*)

STORYTELLER 1: And down.

(*Repeat sound and movement.*)

STORYTELLER 2: He froze.

(SOUND CREW 5 *strikes large drum emphatically.*)

STORYTELLER 3: His body thrust forward. Something was looming.

(SOUND CREW 5 *strikes large drum more emphatically.*)

STORYTELLER 4: Something huge.

(SOUND CREW 5 *strikes large drum and* SOUND CREW 3 *shakes tambourine vigorously, slapping it for emphasis.*)

STORYTELLER 1 (*turning to actors abruptly*): Are you following this?

ALL ACTORS (*nodding*): Yes, keep going.

Scene Three

Characters Storytellers, Coyote, Monster's Eye, Monster's Nostrils, Monster's Mouth

STORYTELLER 2: A huge eyeball appeared.

(SOUND CREW 2 *strikes wood block emphatically as* MONSTER'S EYE 1 *takes position stage left and freezes.*)

STORYTELLER 3: A second eyeball appeared.

(SOUND CREW 2 *strikes wood block emphatically as* MONSTER'S EYE 2 *moves next to* MONSTER'S EYE 1 *and freezes.*)

STORYTELLER 4: Next came two huge, sniffing nostrils.

(SOUND CREW 3 *and* SOUND CREW 5 *scrape sand blocks as sniffing* MONSTER'S NOSTRILS *move, circled arms swinging back and forth, to stand under eyes, and then freeze.*)

STORYTELLER 1: Then came an enormous chewing mouth.

(SOUND CREW 1 *scrapes guiro as* MONSTER'S MOUTH *actors kneel in front and move back and forth, chewing.*)

STORYTELLER 2 (*pointing to face excitedly*): What a face!

COYOTE (*to audience, pointing*): What a face!

STORYTELLER 3: Next came the huge body of many bones and parts.

(SOUND CREW 2 *strikes wood block staccato as each actor rises from their chair and sits cross-legged in a circle on the stage to form* MONSTER'S BODY. *Note:* BODY *actors also play characters inside the* BODY; *they should bring the necessary costume pieces with them.*)

STORYTELLER 4: Coyote stepped forward and bravely called to the monster.

Developing Scripts for Myths and Tales

COYOTE (*cupping paws*): Monster! Oh, Monster!

STORYTELLER 1: Monster's eyes looked.

(SOUND CREW 2 *strikes wood block as pupils of* MONSTER'S EYES *turn, looking.*)

STORYTELLER 2: Monster couldn't see Coyote because Coyote crouched, blending with the scenery.

(COYOTE *crouches to side of stage.*)

STORYTELLER 3: Coyote proposed playing the swallowing game.

COYOTE (*calling*): Monster! Oh, Monster! Swallow me!

STORYTELLER 4: Coyote moved, and the Monster's Eyes saw him.

(SOUND CREW 2 *strikes wood block twice as each* MONSTER EYE *turns and stares at Coyote.*)

STORYTELLER 1: The mouth laughed.

MONSTER'S MOUTH: Ha, ha, ha.

(*All* MONSTER *actors move rhythmically back and forth to simulate laughing.*)

MONSTER'S BODY (*pointing to themselves and then Coyote*): You swallow me first.

STORYTELLER 2: Coyote inhaled with all his might. One, two, three.

COYOTE (*inhaling hugely*): One, two, three.

(SOUND CREW 1 *shakes one rattle each time* COYOTE *inhales.*)

STORYTELLER 3: Then it was Monster's turn. Monster raised his whole body. One, two, three.

MONSTER'S BODY, EYES, NOSTRILS, MOUTH (*raising hands together and inhaling hugely*): One, two, three.

(SOUND CREW 1–5 *shake all rattles emphatically;* SOUND CREW 3 *shakes tambourine emphatically.*)

STORYTELLER 4: Coyote spun around three times.

(SOUND CREW 6 *strikes drum staccato for spinning.* COYOTE *spins in place.*)

STORYTELLER 1: He froze, dizzy.

(SOUND CREW 3 *shakes tambourine and strikes it emphatically.* COYOTE *stops spinning and stumbles.*)

STORYTELLER 2: Seeds underground got yanked up and were scattered hundreds of miles.

(SOUND CREW 3 *shakes tambourine as all* MONSTER *actors mime leaning over and yanking seeds from under the earth and throwing them out to scatter them.*)

STORYTELLER 3: These seeds later became camas roots and berries for people to eat.

Developing Scripts for Myths and Tales

STORYTELLER 4: The force whisked Coyote into Monster's mouth.

(SOUND CREW 1–5 *shake rattles*, SOUND CREW 3 *shakes tambourine*, SOUND CREW 6 *strikes drum staccato as* COYOTE *spins in circles through the* MONSTER'S MOUTH, *landing on the floor inside.*)

STORYTELLER 1: This made Monster's eyes, nose and mouth tired. They closed up and fell asleep.

(SOUND CREW 5 *plays slide whistle as* MONSTER'S EYES, NOSTRILS, *and* MOUTH *sink slowly down, curl up on their sides, and fall asleep.*)

Scene Four

Characters Storytellers, Coyote, Boys, Grizzly Bear, Ledges, Rattlesnake, Brown Bear, People

STORYTELLER 2: Coyote trotted down the throat.

(SOUND CREW 2 *strikes wood block while* COYOTE *trots in place, as if traveling a distance.*)

STORYTELLER 3: He met two boys and put his hands on their shoulders in greeting.

(SOUND CREW 4 *strikes triangle as* BOYS *stand and* COYOTE *greets each.*)

STORYTELLER 4: He asked the way to the heart.

COYOTE: Where's the heart?

STORYTELLER 1: The boys pointed.

(SOUND CREW 4 *strikes triangle as* BOYS *together point toward* HEART *and sit.*)

STORYTELLER 2: Coyote trotted to the heart.

(SOUND CREW 2 *strikes wood block.* COYOTE *continues trotting in place.*)

STORYTELLER 3: But Grizzly Bear raised vicious claws over Coyote.

(SOUND CREW 3 *strikes medium drum as* GRIZZLY BEAR *stands and looms over Coyote.*)

STORYTELLER 4: Coyote loomed over Grizzly Bear.

(SOUND CREW 3 *strikes medium drum as* COYOTE *thrusts forward and* GRIZZLY BEAR *leans back, paws up, retreating. Both freeze.*)

STORYTELLER 1: Grizzly Bear was so surprised by bold Coyote that he fell and cracked his nose on a ledge.

(SOUND CREW 2 *strikes wood block as* LEDGE 1 *appears and* GRIZZLY BEAR *falls back and bangs nose.*)

STORYTELLER 2 (*pointing at* GRIZZLY BEAR): That's why bears have flat noses.

(SOUND CREW 2 *strikes wood block as* GRIZZLY BEAR *stands, faces audience, rubs nose, and sits.*)

STORYTELLER 3: Rattlesnake slithered hissing.

RATTLESNAKE (*slithering and thrusting out head*): Hissss, Hissss, Hisss.

   (SOUND CREW 1 *scrapes guiro for each "hiss" as* RATTLESNAKE *slithers in place on floor.*)

STORYTELLER 4: Coyote called sharply.

COYOTE (*thrusting head forward and pointing*): Don't hiss at me.

   (SOUND CREW 2 *strikes wood block as* RATTLESNAKE *pulls head back, retreating; both freeze.*)

STORYTELLER 1: Rattlesnake was so surprised that he knocked his head on another ledge.

   (SOUND CREW 2 *strikes wood block as* RATTLESNAKE *knocks head on* LEDGE 2.)

STORYTELLER 2 (*pointing*): That's why rattlesnakes have flat heads.

   (SOUND CREW 2 *strikes wood block as* RATTLESNAKE *faces audience, rubs head, and sits.*)

STORYTELLER 3: But helpful Brown Bear pleaded for Coyote to save the People.

BROWN BEAR (*raising paw in greeting*): Please save the People.

STORYTELLER 4: People echoed his words.

PEOPLE 1 (*standing and remaining standing*): Save the people.

PEOPLE 2 (*standing and remaining standing*): Save the people.

PEOPLE 3 (*standing and remaining standing*): Save the people.

PEOPLE 4 (*standing and remaining standing*): Please save the people.

STORYTELLER 1: They cheered, "Coyote."

PEOPLE 1 (*raising arm and cheering*): Coyote.

PEOPLE 2 (*raising arm and cheering*): Coyote.

PEOPLE 3 (*raising arm and cheering*): Coyote.

PEOPLE 4 (*raising arm twice and cheering*): Coyote, Coyote.

STORYTELLER 2: Coyote told them to gather wood.

COYOTE: Gather wood.

   (SOUND CREW 2 *strikes wood block as* COYOTE *points and the* PEOPLE *gather wood.*)

STORYTELLER 3: The People stood behind Coyote and walked toward the heart carrying their wood.

   (SOUND CREW 2 *strikes wood block as* PEOPLE *form a line behind* COYOTE *and all walk in place toward the* HEART.)

Scene Five

Characters Storytellers, Coyote, Monster's Heart, Monster's Heart Thread, People, Red Fire, Smoke, Fox

STORYTELLER 4: The huge heart appeared.

(SOUND CREW 5 *strikes large drum beat emphatically as* MONSTER'S HEART *umbrella pops open dramatically and freezes.*)

MONSTER'S HEART (MONSTER'S BODY *actors rhythmically move hands and body in and out like a heartbeat*): Thump, thump, thump.

(SOUND CREW 5 *strikes large drum powerfully after each thump.*)

STORYTELLER 1: The People put the sticks of wood in a circle.

(SOUND CREW 2 *strikes wood block as the* PEOPLE *mime placing sticks.* RED FIRE *moves to circle of wood sticks, hiding fire until it is lit.*)

STORYTELLER 2: Coyote lit a fire.

(SOUND CREW 1 *strikes guiro as* COYOTE *mimes striking flint and* RED FIRE *leaps up.*)

STORYTELLER 3: The flames leaped.

(SOUND CREW 3 *shakes tambourine as* RED FIRE *dances to indicate a leaping fire.*)

STORYTELLER 4: Smoke circled.

(SOUND CREW 1–5 *shake rattles and* SOUND CREW 3 *shakes tambourine as* SMOKE *actors step into circle, twisting and circling; take time for this effect; after a while,* SOUND CREW 3 *emphatically strikes the center of the tambourine;* SMOKE *actors freeze and then sit.*)

STORYTELLER 1: Monster's mouth coughed.

MONSTER'S EYES, NOSTRILS, MOUTH, BODY ACTORS (*rhythmically thrusting heads forward on each cough*): Cough, cough, cough.

STORYTELLER 2: Nostrils wiggled furiously and sneezed.

MONSTER'S NOSTRILS and BODY (*rhythmically thrusting heads from side to side and sneezing*): Achoo, achoo, achoo.

STORYTELLER 3: Monster's Eyes teared.

MONSTER'S EYES and BODY (*rhythmically moving heads forward and back, holding hands near eyes as if crying*): Boo, hoo, hoo.

STORYTELLER 4: The Monster's Mouth yelled, "Stop!"

MONSTER'S MOUTH and BODY (*loudly and emphatically*): Stop, stop, stop.

STORYTELLER 1: The smoke made Monster sick. He fainted.

(SOUND CREW 5 *plays slide whistle as* MONSTER BODY *and* FACE *actors slowly lie down on their sides and then freeze with legs tucked up.*)

STORYTELLER 2: But Monster's evil heart still thumped.

MONSTER'S HEART, EYES, NOSTRILS, MOUTH, BODY ACTORS (*loudly, from their reclining positions*): Thump. Thump. Thump.

(SOUND CREW 5 *strikes large drum after each thump.*)

STORYTELLER 3: Coyote must destroy the evil heart.

COYOTE (*raising hand to audience*): I must destroy the evil heart!

STORYTELLER 4: He lifted a stone knife and cut at the heart once.

(SOUND CREW 1 *scrapes guiro once as* COYOTE *mimes one cut.*)

STORYTELLER 1: But the knife broke, and Coyote tossed it away.

(SOUND CREW 2 *strikes wood block as* COYOTE *tosses it away.*)

STORYTELLER 2: Coyote took his second knife and cut twice. But the knife broke and Coyote tossed it away.

(SOUND CREW 1 *scrapes guiro twice as* COYOTE *makes two cuts.* SOUND CREW 2 *strikes wood block for tossing knife away.*)

STORYTELLER 3: Coyote took a third knife and cut three times. The knife broke.

(SOUND CREW 1 *scrapes guiro three times as* COYOTE *makes three cuts.* SOUND CREW 2 *strikes wood block for tossing knife away.*)

STORYTELLER 4: Coyote took a fourth knife and cut four times, but the knife broke.

(SOUND CREW 1 *scrapes guiro four times.* SOUND CREW 2 *strikes wood block for tossing knife away.*)

STORYTELLER 1: Coyote took his fifth and last knife and cut five times, but the knife broke.

(SOUND CREW 1 *scrapes guiro five times.* SOUND CREW 2 *strikes wood block for tossing knife away.*)

STORYTELLER 2: The heart held on by one thread.

(SOUND CREW 4 *strikes triangle as* HEART THREAD *displays the red ribbon of the heart thread.*)

STORYTELLER 3: Coyote grabbed the thread and pulled and pulled and pulled.

(SOUND CREW 1–5 *shake rattles.* SOUND CREW 3 *shakes tambourine.* SOUND CREW 6 *strikes drum staccato to build tension as* COYOTE *pretends to pull thread with all his might.*)

STORYTELLER 4: It broke.

(SOUND CREW 3 *strikes medium drum emphatically as both* MONSTER HEART *and* COYOTE *fall down in slow motion.*)

STORYTELLER 1: Monster writhed and groaned in agony.

(SOUND CREW 1–5 *shake rattles.* SOUND CREW 3 *shakes tambourine as* MONSTER *actors writhe and groan.*)

Developing Scripts for Myths and Tales

STORYTELLER 2: Monster keeled over dead.

(SOUND CREW 5 *strikes large drum most emphatically and* SOUND CREW 3 *strikes tambourine emphatically in center as* MONSTER *actors freeze.*)

STORYTELLER 3: Only the face remained alive.

STORYTELLER 4: Coyote ordered everyone to go to the mouth to escape.

COYOTE (*pointing*): Go to the mouth and escape fast.

STORYTELLER 1: They climbed out rapidly.

(SOUND CREW 2 *strikes wood block as the* FOUR PEOPLE *and* FOX *step through the mouth and form a line downstage left. The rest remain lying down.*)

Scene Six

Characters Storytellers, Coyote, Muskrat, Eyes, Mouth, Nostrils, Fox, People, Color White, Color Green, Color Black, Color Gold

STORYTELLER 2: The mouth closed up, but Muskrat was still inside.

COYOTE (*hands on hips*): Muskrat, what are you doing? Hurry up.

STORYTELLER 3: Muskrat's head poked through the left nostril.

(SOUND CREW 2 *strikes wood block as* MUSKRAT *pokes head through triangular opening of* MONSTER'S NOSTRIL.)

STORYTELLER 4: His body squeezed through.

(SOUND CREW 2 *strikes wood block as* MUSKRAT *stands and squeezes through to waist.*)

STORYTELLER 1: But the nostril closed, and Muskrat's tail was inside.

(NOSTRIL *actor closes arms around Muskrat.*)

STORYTELLER 2: Coyote ordered everyone to pull.

COYOTE (*intensely*): Pull.

STORYTELLER 3: Fox and the People formed a line and pulled—one, two, three.

COYOTE, FOX, and PEOPLE (*pulling in slow motion, exerting energy*): One, two, three.

(SOUND CREW 3 *shakes tambourine, creating the pulling tension.*)

STORYTELLER 4: Out popped Muskrat.

(SOUND CREW 3 *strikes tambourine emphatically in center as* MUSKRAT *falls on floor in slow motion in one direction and the others fall in the other direction.*)

STORYTELLER 1: Muskrat examined his tail. The hair was all scraped off.

MUSKRAT (*looking at tail, to audience, horrified*): My hair!

COYOTE (*hands on hips*): That's what you get for being late.

(SOUND CREW 2 *strikes wood block.*)

STORYTELLER 2 (*pointing to tail*): That's why muskrats have bare tails.

(*SOUND CREW 2 strikes wood block as* MUSKRAT, *facing audience, holds tail up, examines it, and shakes head.*)

STORYTELLER 3: Coyote had the People gather stone knives to participate in the carving of the Monster.

COYOTE: Gather knives.

(*SOUND CREW 2 strikes wood block as the* PEOPLE *pick up knives.*)

STORYTELLER 4: Everyone carved.

(*SOUND CREW 1 scrapes guiro as the* PEOPLE *carve.*)

STORYTELLER 1: Coyote dealt out portions of the body to different parts of the country.

(*The* PEOPLE *and* FOX *sit cross-legged downstage left to observe.*)

STORYTELLER 2: By this act, he showed where each tribe of people would live.

STORYTELLER 3: Some body parts spun North.

(*SOUND CREW 6 strikes high piano notes as* COYOTE *gestures toward one group of actors—the northern tribe, including* COLOR WHITE *and* BUFFALO—*who rise, circle in slow motion up center, and freeze.* COYOTE *poses with them, hands out in gesture of presentation.*)

STORYTELLER 4: This is White.

(*SOUND CREW 6 strikes one emphatic high piano note as* COLOR WHITE *ceremonially raises white banner.*)

STORYTELLER 1: The Color of Wisdom.

(*Actors representing northern tribe look up, freezing to indicate higher wisdom.*)

STORYTELLER 2: Its animal is Buffalo.

(*SOUND CREW 6 strikes high piano note as* BUFFALO *takes stylized, powerful buffalo position and freezes.*)

STORYTELLER 3: Parts spun South.

(*SOUND CREW 6 strikes low piano notes as* COYOTE *gestures to southern tribe, including* COLOR GREEN *and* MOUSE, *who stand and slowly circle downstage. They kneel and freeze.* COYOTE *stands by them in gesture of presentation.*)

STORYTELLER 4: This is Green.

(*SOUND CREW 6 strikes one low piano note as* COLOR GREEN *displays green banner.*)

STORYTELLER 1: The place of Innocence and Trust.

(*SOUND CREW 6 strikes low piano note as southern tribe actors look to the side or with eyes downcast to show innocence.*)

STORYTELLER 2: Its animal is Mouse.

(SOUND CREW 6 strikes low piano note as MOUSE pops up, taking small, tucked-in mouse posture with paws near face; COYOTE stands with them, freezing in a gesture of presentation.)

STORYTELLER 3: Parts spun West.

(SOUND CREW 6 strikes medium low piano notes as COYOTE gestures to western tribe,
including COLOR BLACK and BEAR, who turn in stylized, slow circles to stage left and freeze.
COYOTE stands with them, freezing in a gesture of presentation.)

STORYTELLER 4: This is Black.

(SOUND CREW 6 strikes one medium low piano note as COLOR BLACK stands, displays black
banner, and freezes.)

STORYTELLER 1: The Place of Quiet Thinking.

(SOUND CREW 6 strikes medium low piano note as western tribe actors put hands under chins or
make other gestures indicating thinking.)

STORYTELLER 2: Its animal is Bear.

(SOUND CREW 6 strikes one emphatic medium low piano note as BEAR takes powerful bear position, perhaps with paws above head, and freezes. COYOTE stands to the side, freezing in a gesture
of presentation.)

STORYTELLER 3: The last parts spun East.

(SOUND CREW 6 strikes medium high piano note as COYOTE gestures to the eastern tribe, including COLOR GOLD and EAGLE, who circle stage right and freeze. COYOTE stands near them,
freezing in a gesture of presentation.)

STORYTELLER 4: This is Gold.

(SOUND CREW 6 strikes one emphatic medium high piano note as COLOR GOLD displays
banner and freezes.)

STORYTELLER 1: The place of Illumination and Light.

(Eastern tribe actors look up and raise hands.)

STORYTELLER 2: Its animal is Eagle.

(SOUND CREW 6 strikes emphatic medium high piano note as EAGLE kneels in profile with wings
outstretched and head thrust up proudly. COYOTE stands to the side, freezing in a gesture of
presentation.)

STORYTELLER 3: Coyote named the tribes that would live in the different parts.
Some were called...

STORYTELLER 3 (pointing North): Sioux.

STORYTELLER 3 (pointing South): Navajo.

STORYTELLER 3 (*pointing West*): Apache.

STORYTELLER 3 (*pointing East*): Abenaki and many others.

STORYTELLER 4: But Fox raised a paw. Coyote forgot to name the People here.

FOX (*alarmed, pointing to the* FOUR PEOPLE): You forgot us.

STORYTELLER 1: Coyote paced back and forth.

(SOUND CREW 2 *strikes wood block for pacing.*)

COYOTE (*shaking head*): I forgot.

STORYTELLER 2: Coyote washed his hands, covered with blood from Monster.

(SOUND CREW 4 *strikes triangle as* COYOTE *mimes washing hands.*)

STORYTELLER 3 (*pointing to floor*): He sprinkled the bloody water right here, on the plateau.

(SOUND CREW 4 *rings bell for sprinkling water.*)

STORYTELLER 4: And he named the people here the Nez Percé tribe.

COYOTE (*sprinkling water on the* PEOPLE): You will be the Nez Percé. You will be little people but very powerful and strong.

STORYTELLER 1: The Nez Percé stood proudly. They aimed their bows and arrows and shot. They hit the mark.

(SOUND CREW 2 *strikes wood block as the* FOUR PEOPLE *mime shooting arrows.*)

STORYTELLER 2: The People bowed in thanks to Coyote. They presented him with a ceremonial staff.

(PEOPLE 2, PEOPLE 3, *and* PEOPLE 4 *bow deeply;* PEOPLE 1 *hands staff to* COYOTE *who freezes, holding it up.*)

STORYTELLER 3: They did a dance of thanksgiving to Coyote for freeing them from the Monster.32

STORYTELLER 4: And Coyote danced, too. For soon would come the beginning of the human race.

(SOUND CREW 1 *plays taped music and performers perform the Native American dance from the beginning of the play.* COYOTE *dances in the center, perhaps doing the Tap step, circling in place and moving his ceremonial staff rhythmically.*)

Developing Scripts for Myths and Tales

Finale

STORYTELLER 1: Thank you students, adults, too.

STORYTELLER 2: For letting us share our story with you.

STORYTELLER 3: Of a Nez Percé myth, old yet new.

STORYTELLER 4: We hope it came alive for you.

STORYTELLER 1: And here's a last tip from us, your friends.

STORYTELLER 2 (*holding up book of Native American myths*): Read a book of these myths from beginning to end.

STORYTELLER 3: And study different cultures wherever they may be.

STORYTELLER 4: For the more that you know, the more you'll be...

(STORYTELLERS *gesture to all performers.*)

EVERYONE (*making big circular gesture around their heads*): Free!

STORYTELLER 1: The actors are...

STORYTELLER 2: The Sound Crew is...

STORYTELLER 3: The Storytellers are...

STORYTELLER 4: Thank you.

To end the performance, STORYTELLERS 1–4 *introduce the performers, having them stand and say their names loudly and clearly. When all are standing,* STORYTELLERS 1–4 *turn toward them and raise arms. Everyone follows, raising their arms and bringing them down together for a group bow, saying "Thank you" as they do so. Performers then sit for the audience performance discussion.*

Story Questions and Research Topics

To spark students' interest and enrich the cultural experience, provide a variety of materials for investigation, dramatic play, study, and observation. Suggestions include artifacts, clothing, utensils, photographs, artwork, and books. Discussion questions and research topics can be pursued before embarking on a drama experience, during play rehearsal, or after the production to support the culture being introduced.

Story Questions

1. Describe the characteristics of Coyote. Would you like him as a friend? Explain.

2. Coyote is the hero of this story, but sometimes he makes mistakes. What mistakes does he make? Why do you think many Native North American Indian tribes make Coyote their hero even though he makes mistakes?

3. Who is the villain in this story? What does he do? Why do you think he acts the way he does? What is he trying to achieve?

4. Why do the storytellers ask, "What will you give us for our story?" Why don't they tell stories for free?

5. Coyote is known as a trickster hero. Whom does he trick and how? What does he do that is heroic?

6. What does Coyote do that shows he has confidence?

7. One purpose of Native North American Indian storytelling is to teach children a tribe's origins or early beginnings and how to behave. What might Nez Percé children learn about their origins from this story? What might they learn about behavior?

8. Coyote is called a culture hero, meaning that many Native North American Indian groups have chosen him as their hero. Why do you think so many chose a coyote over some other animal? What qualities make the coyote an interesting choice for a hero?

9. Native North American Indian stories of Coyote often have lots of humor. What funny things happen in this story?

10. Where in the story does Coyote act like a person and where does he act like an animal? What might be the advantages if you were able to have the qualities of both a coyote and a person? What could you do that you cannot do now?

11. In the early history of Native North American Indians, what was best for the group was most important. How does this story show that the welfare of the group is most important?

12. Native North American Indian stories are often set in one of three ages—the Myth Age, when no humans lived; the Transformation Age, when people were new to the earth and someone was helping them; and the Historical Age, when people began making history. In what age does this story take place? Why do you think so?

Theater-Performance Questions

1. Native North American Indian storytellers often use big gestures, facial expressions, and voice changes to become the characters in a story. How would this keep an audience's attention?

2. Native North American Indian storytellers often break off in the middle of a story to ask, "Are you following this?" and then wait for the audience's response. Why do you think storytellers do this? How might this help keep the audience's attention?

3. Singing and dancing are sacred and religious to Native North American Indians. How, then, might Native North American Indians feel about those who dance their dances in a wild or out-of-control manner? In what way should these dances be performed?

4. Drumming is an important element of Native North American Indian music. What in nature might the sound of a drum represent? Experiment making sound effects using only a drum. Native North American Indians have a type of drumming called *thunder drumming*, in which drums are played rapidly or staccato. Practice thunder drumming. In what parts of this play might thunder drumming be effective?

Research Topics

1. Traditionally, Native North American Indians often told stories in winter, when, as the Pueblo say, "the earth goes to sleep." What makes the winter an ideal time for storytelling?

2. Often a trickster fools his enemy, but sometimes the trickster himself gets tricked. Find a story in which Coyote gets tricked.

3. Coyote is a culture hero for the Nez Percé, one of the Northern Mountain Plateau/Pacific Coast tribes. He is also in the tales of groups from the southwestern deserts and mountains, and from California. Other groups have different culture heroes. Research these heroes. Why might some groups have chosen animals other than the coyote?

4. In Native North American Indian culture, an old woman, often a grandmother, is the storyteller. What might be the advantage of having an old woman rather than a young one tell these stories?

5. Why do you think the Native North American Indians used colors to represent the four directions? What might people learn from this?

6. Many older Native North American Indians are concerned that some of the younger generation are not interested in traditional legends and myths. What is lost if the stories of their early history and ancestors are not passed on to the next generation?

7. Why do you think there is a renewed interest in Native North American Indian culture?

8. What does it mean to say that the Native North American Indians are at home in nature?

9. An important ritual for Native North American Indians is "the vision quest," when a young person (ten or eleven years old) travels into the wilderness seeking their guardian spirit. The guardian spirit usually appears in the form of an animal. If you were to have an animal spirit helper, what would you want it to be? What do you appreciate and value in that animal? Why is it special for you?

10. Why have Native North American Indians been called the first ecologists?

11. Native North American Indians often sit in a circle during meetings, story-telling, and religious ceremonies. Traditional objects and forms, including te-pees, medicine wheels, and shields, are often circular. Why is the circle so important? What does the circle represent? Research to learn more about the Sacred Circle.

12. Traditionally, Native North American Indian art was not meant for museums but was used to decorate rugs, buffalo robes, tepee walls, war shields, baskets, and saddlebags and other leather items. Today, more and more Native Americans are creating art for museums as well as for personal use. Find examples of this beautiful art. What is the value of decorating things that you wear or use? What is the value of creating art for display in museums?

13. Many books have been written about Chief Joseph, a wise and great Nez Percé chief. Find out what Chief Joseph did that made him a great hero.

Selected Bibliography
Native North American Indian Stories

Bierhorst, John. *Doctor Coyote; A Native American Aesop's Fables.* Illustrated by Wendy Watson. New York: Macmillan, Inc., 1987. Contemporary retellings of Aesop's fables originally told by Aztec Indians in the 1500s, with Coyote as the main character.

Bruchac, Joseph. *Native American Stories.* Golden, CO: Fulcrum Publishing, 1991. A book of Native North American Indian lessons from many tribes, divided into categories.

Bruchac, Joseph, and Jonathan London. *Thirteen Moons on Turtle's Back; A Native American Year of Moons.* Illustrated by Thomas Locker. New York: Philomel Books, 1992. Poetic retellings of the meaning of the thirteen moons in different Native American tribes. Each would be easy to dramatize.

Clark, Ella. *Indian Legends from the Northern Rockies.* Norman, OK: University of Oklahoma Press, 1966. Excellent book for older students, featuring myths and fascinating information that is presented clearly and succinctly.

Curry, Louise. *Back in the Beforetime; Tales of the California Indians.* Illustrated by James Watts. New York: Margaret K. McElderry Books, 1987. Animal creation and trickster tales, often featuring Coyote. Appeals to age nine and above.

Goble, Paul. *Crow Chief; A Plains Indian Story.* New York: Orchard Books, 1992. Beautifully illustrated story of the Buffalo Hunt. Good to dramatize.

————. *The Gift of the Sacred Dog*. New York: Macmillan, Inc., 1980. A beautifully illustrated Plains story. Includes a depiction of the buffalo dance.

————. *The Girl Who Loved Wild Horses*. New York: Bradbury Press, 1978. Caldecott medal winner. Poignant story of a Native American girl who is destined to follow the horses because of her special identification with them.

Goble, Paul, and Dorothy Goble. *The Friendly Wolf*. New York: Bradbury Press, 1974. A wonderful example of the awe and respect felt by Native Americans for the beauty and power of nature. This book explains why Native Americans consider wolves to be their friends. Beautiful, evocative art.

Haviland, Virginia, ed. *North American Legends*. New York: Collins, 1979. Includes tales told by European and African immigrants and by Native North American Indians and Eskimos.

McDermott, Gerald. *Arrow to the Sun; A Pueblo Indian Tale*. New York: Viking Press, 1974. Winner of the Caldecott medal and illustrated with authentic Pueblo designs. An exciting story that is good to dramatize.

————. *Raven; A Trickster Tale from the Pacific Northwest*. San Diego: Harcourt Brace Jovanovich, 1993. A retelling of how the trickster, Raven, brought light to the world. Magnificently illustrated in authentic Pacific Northwest style.

Oughton, Jerrie. *How the Stars Fell into the Sky; A Navajo Legend*. Illustrated by Lisa Desimini. Boston: Houghton Mifflin, 1992. A beautiful rendering of the story of why stars are scattered throughout the sky. Lush art will appeal to all ages. Could easily be dramatized.

Wood, Marion. *Spirits, Heroes and Hunters from North American Indian Mythology*. Illustrated by John Sibbick. New York: Schocken Books, 1981. Myths and stories from many tribes, including background information with each story. Richly illustrated. For students age ten and above.

Coyote Stories

Baker, Betty. *And Me, Coyote!* Illustrated by Maria Horvath. New York: Macmillan, Inc., 1982. Charming adaptation of Coyote creation myths of central and southern California. Captures the magical and humorous feeling of the stories.

Begay, Shonto. *Maii and Cousin, Horned Toad*. New York: Scholastic, Inc., 1992. Maii, the coyote, is always hungry and greedy. He eats the corn belonging to his hardworking toad and then swallows the toad, only to experience the dire results of his actions. Adapted by a Navajo writer, the humorous text includes Native North American Indian words and songs, with a glossary describing their meaning and how to pronounce them.

Martin, Fran. *Nine Tales of Coyote*. New York: Harper, 1950. Lively retellings of mostly Nez Percé Coyote tales, including "The Kamiah Monster," are dramatized in this book.

Reed, Evelyn Dahl. *Coyote Tales from the Indian Pueblos*. Santa Fe, NM: Sunstone Press, 1988. Coyote tales from several tribes. Appeals to students age nine and older, with helpful pictures showing the many sides of Coyote's personality.

Robinson, Gail, and Douglas Hill. *Coyote, the Trickster.* New York: Crane Russak, 1976. Coyote and Raven stories from different tribes for grade four and above. Several stories are short and good to dramatize.

Performance

Bierhorst, John. *A Cry From the Earth; Music of the North American Indians.* New York: Four Winds Press, 1979. A noted scholar provides authentic photos of Native North American Indians in traditional costume, together with their instruments.

Powers, William K. *Indian Dancing and Costumes.* New York: Putnam, 1966. This book provides clear descriptions of types of dances, dance steps, and costuming.

Showers, Paul. *Indian Festivals.* New York: Thomas Y. Crowell Company, 1969. Informative, authentic picture book describing Native North American Indian festivals and focusing on dance.

Cultural Information

Bierhorst, John, ed. *Lightning Inside You and Other Native American Riddles.* New York: William Morrow & Co., 1992. Native North American Indian, Mexican, and Mayan riddles divided into categories. How these games tie into the life and customs of the people is also described.

Caduto, Michael J., and Joseph Bruchac. *Keepers of the Earth; Native American Stories and Environmental Activities for Children.* Golden, CO: Fulcrum Publishing. Stories from different tribes. Questions on the stories and environmental activities for different age levels are described.

Freedman, Russell. *Buffalo Hunt.* New York: Holiday House, 1988. Detailed description of the buffalo hunt and related religious ceremonies and rituals. Richly illustrated with paintings by nineteenth-century artists who witnessed it.

Fronval, George, and Daniel Dubois. *Indian Signs and Signals.* New York: Sterling Publishing Co., Inc., 1981. This fascinating book of Native North American Indian sign language includes smoke signals and the language of feathers and blankets. Appealing to all ages and a good supplement for dramatization.

Hook, Jason. *Chief Joseph, Guardian of the Nez Percé.* New York: Firebird Books, 1989. Background information on the Nez Percé provides the setting for the inspiring story of Chief Joseph, showing the wisdom and compassion of this great leader.

Trafzer, Clifford E. *The Nez Percé.* New York: Chelsea House, 1992. One of a series of books focusing on different tribes. Valuable information on the Nez Percé, including the origin of the Coyote story.

CHAPTER EIGHT

The Crane Maiden

A Traditional Japanese Folk Tale

This tale is a favorite in Japan. There are many written versions of it and it has been adapted into plays, a movie, and an opera. Every year, Japanese parents read the story to their children and take them to see some version of it. It is called a transformation tale. Transformation tales are stories in which an animal transforms *into a person and back into an animal again. They are common in Japan.*

The tale tells the story of a poor old man and old woman who lived in a hut in the forest a long, long time ago. On a freezing winter day, the old man trudged outside into the snow to gather twigs for their fire. While searching for twigs, he discovered a beautiful crane stuck in the arms of a steel trap. The old man freed the crane from the trap, and it flew away. On his way back to the hut, the old man miraculously found twigs that had not been there before. The old man told the story of the crane to his wife, and the two prayed for the safety of the bird. After a short time, a maiden who had lost her way in the forest appeared at the hut. Being generous people, the couple invited the maiden to stay with them. During the night, the maiden used an old loom to weave a beautiful cloth which she gave to the couple. She told them to sell the cloth so they would no longer be poor. The couple were grateful but could not part with the precious gift. The maiden decided to weave a second piece of cloth for them to sell. Before doing so, the maiden asked the couple to promise never to look at her while she was weaving. They agreed. But they were unusually curious, and when they peeked over the screen that hid the maiden, the couple discovered a beautiful crane weaving feathers on the loom! Startled at having been discovered, the crane dropped her feathers and flew out the door. This was the crane that the old man had rescued! Months passed and as spring approached, the couple heard the familiar sound of flying cranes. As they looked into the sky, they saw their crane maiden friend, who had come to say a final good-bye.

Acting Exercises

The following acting exercises may be used to help students practice acting principles and develop the characters that make up the cast of this play.

Experiencing Cultural Customs

Goal   To practice Japanese customs: bowing, sitting on heels, eating rice.

Acting Principle   Belief.

Optional Materials   Small rice bowl, chopsticks.

Procedure   Explain that in Japan people bow instead of shake hands as a gesture of greeting. Bow to the person next to you. Now shake their hand. How are these gestures different? People of the same social level bow at the same level. Can you imagine why? How low would a subject bow to a ruler? Explain that students will practice bowing as well as eating (show rice bowl and chopsticks) and kneeling while they act out the following short scenes from the story. Everyone participates.

- You are the old man or woman. Wake up in the morning. Stretch to get the kinks out. Bow to each other and then to the East to show gratitude to the gods for your life.
- Walk in place to the hearth and bow to the hearth gods by clapping twice to awaken the god within, bowing your head in prayer, and wishing for something special.
- Kneel by the hearth, sitting back on your heels. Pick up a rice bowl. Show its size. Pick up chopsticks and slowly eat each grain. Freeze. Discuss how eating rice in a small bowl with chopsticks is different from eating rice with a fork or spoon.

Practicing Japanese Movement Styles

Goal   To teach movement styles used in Japanese theatre that will help students enact the characters.

Acting Principle   Belief.

Procedure   Explain that Japanese theatre is highly stylized and that each character has a definite movement style. Have students try the movement styles below.

- Man's movement: Make your body look as square and large as possible. Turn toes out and stand with legs apart. Stride in place with arms held away from the body.
- Woman's movement: Make your body look as feminine and graceful as possible. Hold your knees together. Turn toes slightly inward. Glide as you move (but don't slide), picking up each foot but taking small steps to accommodate a tight kimono. Turn and try to make your body look like the shape of the letter *S*. Walk tall, as if a string is pulling from the top of your head. Freeze. Tilt your head for accent. Hold hands together in a position of prayer or modestly fold them in front of you, with your elbows held away from your body.
- Objects: Walk heel-toe-heel-toe with a slight shuffle. Freeze. Always look down when standing in a neutral position.

Enacting Scenes Using the "Mie" Technique

Goal To practice the *mie* (pronounced me-ay), an important Japanese theatre technique and convention used in this play.

Acting Principles Voice and Movement, Control.

Procedure Explain that *mie* is an important acting technique. The actor uses the whole face and body to show a strong emotion and then freezes so that the audience can focus on the expression. Practice the following scenes using the *mie* technique:

- The crane caught in the trap.
- The old man seeing the crane's distress.
- The couple seeing the mysterious maiden at their humble door.
- The couple's reaction to the magnificent cloth.
- The Crane Maiden realizing the couple has peeked while she is weaving.
- The couple's remorse that they peeked.
- The Crane Maiden leaving the old couple to fly off forever.
- The couple's reaction as the Crane Maiden flies off.

Enacting the Objects

Goal To introduce the Prop People, a Japanese theatre convention.

Acting Principle Belief.

Procedure Explain that in Japanese and Chinese theatre, scenery and minor characters are often played by Prop People who are dressed in black so as to appear invisible to the audience. They sometimes manipulate materials as scenery or they may become the scenery itself. They also hand props to the actors. Students can practice being Prop People, transforming themselves from one object to another and freezing after creating each one. Objects are swirling snow, pines with tall tops blowing in the wind, a trap with cruel steel jaws opened to capture the crane, a loom for the crane's weaving, a cherry tree displaying beautiful blossoms of spring.

Becoming the Crane and the Maiden

Goal To use stylized Japanese movements to depict the Crane Maiden.

Acting Principles Belief, Voice and Movement.

Procedure Show students pictures of the Crane Maiden from this book and others (see *Bibliography*). Explain that they will first become a crane and then transform themselves into the Maiden. Explain that in Japan, an actor playing a bird keeps arms straight and thumbs tucked under. Also mention that men play women's roles in Japanese Kabuki theatre.

- Begin as a crane at rest with wings at your sides. Push off the ground with your big, strong claws. Flap your huge wings. Soar, sweeping your wings through the sky. Show their size by making big, clear, slow sweeping motions. Land. Feel the jaws of a steel trap grab your leg. Freeze, showing your pain. A man pries you free. Turn to him and show gratitude. Limp away. Then push off again and fly into the air. Freeze.

- Become an elegant Japanese maiden, graceful and delicate. Walk tall with small steps, toes slightly inward, legs close together. Feel as if a string is stretching up through your head to make you look as tall as possible. Bring your hands up in a position of prayer to create a beautiful silhouette. Now turn and make your body look like the letter *S* so that you look as graceful as possible. Tilt head to side. Freeze, creating a posed picture of the graceful Japanese maiden.

Sweeping the Floor in Slow Motion

Goal   To enact a clear, stylized pantomime.

Acting Principle   Belief.

Procedure   Discuss how clear mime is essential to Japanese theatre. Explain that students will pretend to sweep the floor in slow motion to emphasize its essential actions. Everyone participates. Reach for an imaginary straw broom. Show the thickness of the handle and how it is held. Feel its weight. Examine the room. Which part needs sweeping the most? Walk in place to that area. Sweep carefully, showing the force needed to make the floor spotless. Open an imaginary door. Sweep all of the offending dust outside. Get each speck. Put the broom back against the wall. Freeze, examining your work. Use clear pantomime to show other such actions from the play.

Enacting the Old Man's Adventure

Goal   Miming the old man's actions.

Acting Principle   Belief.

Procedure   Discuss the importance of actors believing in the actions they are performing in order to make them seem real. This is a good activity to lessen self consciousness and get students' creative juices going.

Become the old man. Reach down and pick up a heavy harness to carry sticks and put it on carefully. Walk in place with open, wide steps to the door and open it. Feel the blast of icy air bite into your face. React. Then trudge one foot after another in place through the deep snow. Your foot sinks deeper and deeper as you go further into the forest. See the crane struggling in the trap. React and freeze. Reach down and exert energy to pry the jaws of the trap apart. Reach out to help the crane. Watch as she flies away. Trudge home. Discover the pile of twigs miraculously placed by the door. Pick up the twigs, one by one. Open the door and go quickly inside. Show the twigs to the old woman. Freeze.

Production Notes

The following guidelines may be used to enhance the quality of the production with dance movements and simple costumes.

Japanese Crane Dance

Music   "Sakura" (the Cherry Blossoms), from the audio tape entitled *Japanese Masterpieces for the Koto*. Lyrichord Discs, Inc., 142 Perry Street, New York, NY, 10014.

Purpose and Style   To show the essence of the crane and its movements. Needs a clean, stylized quality.

Materials   Japanese obis (sashes) or silk scarves representing obis can be fastened around waists. Dance fans can be used as wings.

Formation   A straight line facing the audience; movement is forward and back. Two lead dancers initiate the actions and the rest follow. Use at least four dancers.

Steps and Stances   Steps are small. The foot glides and is picked up but does not slide. Repeat sequences or multiples of four beats or steps. All movements begin on left foot. Fingers are held together with thumbs tucked under. To depict flapping wings, arms are held straight and rigid; the elbow does not bend. Dancers move and then freeze or pose, creating a still picture.

> *Step One:* The two lead dancers stand upstage, one on each side. The other dancers stand in a line between them. The main leader is stage right. Dancers wait for music to begin, with their backs to the audience and fans concealed. Music begins and dancers dramatically open their fans, turn slightly to the left, and create an *S* shape with their bodies. They pose, revealing only their eyes above the fan.

Step One

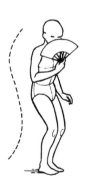

Step Two: Lead dancer waits a few beats and then begins the Lifting Wings step, moving forward on left foot; the others follow. Leader takes four small steps, slowly raising arms but keeping them rigid. On step four, the leader poses with toe pointing down, wings raised.

Lifting Wings Step

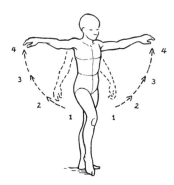

Step Three: Leader moves forward again in the Pushing Wings Down step. On the fourth and final beat, the leader poses with wings lowered. Repeat the Lifting Wings and Pushing Wings Down steps until dancers reach downstage.

Pushing Wings Down Step

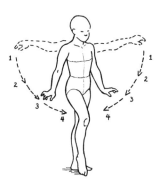

Step Four: Beginning on the left foot, dancers turn slightly to create an *S* shape and use their hands for the Pushing Air Away From the Body step on a count of four beats. They move backward one step as they mime pushing air away from their bodies, silently counting "push, two, three, four." The pushing motion is repeated to the right and then to the left until the dancers reach upstage. Pose in *S* shape, pushing.

Pushing Air Away From the Body Step

Step Five: Dancers stay in place for the step. Dancers pretend to grasp a big feather between middle finger and thumb with left hand. They lift the feather up in front of their faces and let it drop, repeating the step with right hand. This should have a flowing, weaving motion as dancers repeat lifting the feather, first in one hand and then the other, eight times.

Step Five

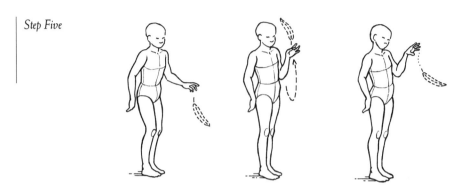

Step Six: For the Washing Silk in the River step, dancers stay upstage in place, face left, and pretend to hold in both hands a piece of silk. To a count of four, dancers turn slightly to the left and swish the cloth on that side. They then turn to the right and swish the cloth on that side. The motions are repeated four times.

Washing Silk in the River Step

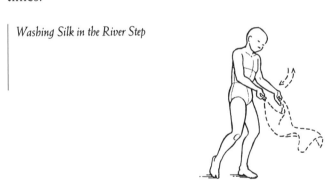

When steps are completed, the leader poses in an *S* shape with eyes revealed above the fan. The music fades. Fans are dramatically snapped shut, and dancers move with erect postures to their chairs, where they quickly remove costume pieces.

Finale: The final dance at the conclusion of the play is the same as the opening dance.

Costume Suggestions

For narrative mime presentations, all students wear black clothing—black shirts and black pants—with individual character costumes worn as additional pieces to the all-black attire.

Storytellers Hapi coats (short kimonos) that may be constructed from varying or identical fabric. Alternatively, Storytellers might wear full-length kimonos. Kimonos may easily be adapted from bathrobe patterns. White headbands.

Old Man   Baggy black pants, hapi coat, cone-shaped straw hat with cord for attaching under chin.

Old Woman   Baggy black pants, hapi coat that is not the same color as that of the Old Man.

Crane Maiden   A strip of white fabric about forty-eight inches long and twelve inches wide may be placed around shoulders and held at each end to resemble wings for the Crane. A red headband about one inch wide may be worn to represent the red crest. A white kimono with black trim on the sleeves and a bright red obi or sash may be worn for the Maiden.

Peaked Hut Roof   No costume other than black clothing is necessary. Actors use their bodies to form a roof shape.

Hearth   No costume other than black clothing is necessary. Actor uses body to form the rounded shape of a hearth.

Fire   Two dowels about eighteen inches long with gold tinsel or gold ribbons attached. Two similar dowels with red tinsel ribbons or strips of crepe paper.

Swirling Snow   Two eighteen-inch dowels for each Snow actor with strips of white crepe paper attached.

Pines   No costume other than black clothing is necessary.

Mist   Three yards of thirty-six-inch wide white nylon netting held across the stage.

Steel Trap   No costume other than black clothing is necessary. Actors use their bodies to form a trap shape.

Crane   A strip of white fabric about forty-eight inches long and twelve inches wide may be placed around shoulders and held at each end to resemble wings. A red headband may be worn to represent the red crest.

Japanese Screen   Cream-colored or beige material with bamboo or a stylized Japanese pine tree drawn in black marker; any plain, opaque fabric; or any fabric with a Japanese design.

Cherry Tree   Two bouquets of artificial flowers with big pink blooms for each Tree. If artificial flowers are unavailable, flowers can be created from pink tissue or crepe paper.

The Crane Maiden

A Traditional Japanese Folk Tale

⊗ ≈⊗≈ ⊗ ≈⊗≈ ⊗ ≈⊗≈ ⊗ ≈⊗≈ ⊗ ≈⊗≈ ⊗ ≈⊗≈ ⊗

Cast

FOUR STORYTELLERS (strong, bright, enthusiastic voices and gestures)

OLD MAN (strong and vigorous but humble; walks close to the earth)

OLD WOMAN (strong, humble, hard working)

CRANE MAIDEN (graceful fluttering movements as crane; tall, aristocratic posture as the maiden, with small steps and movements)

PEAKED HUT ROOF (2)

HEARTH

FIRE

SWIRLING SNOW (3)

PINE (3)

MIST (4)

STEEL TRAP (2)

CRANE (4)

JAPANESE SCREEN (2)

LOOM (2)

CHERRY TREE (7)

Adaptations   The number of objects and cranes appearing in the production can be adapted to meet the needs of your classroom; add more for large classes and reduce the number of actors for small classes.

$\otimes \approx\otimes\approx \otimes \approx\otimes\approx \otimes \approx\otimes\approx \otimes \approx\otimes\approx \otimes \approx\otimes\approx \otimes \approx\otimes\approx \otimes$

Sound Crew

While suggestions are made here, other instruments or instruments made from "found objects" might be added or substituted, as necessary. (See *Setting the Scene*, Chapter Two, for suggestions.)

SOUND CREW 1	taped Japanese music, piano or resonator bells (does not need to know how to play the piano), rattle
SOUND CREW 2	piano or resonator bells, guiro, rattle
SOUND CREW 3	gong (played by hitting small cymbal with padded drumstick), rattle, tambourine
SOUND CREW 4	wood block
SOUND CREW 5	triangle, sand blocks, rattle
SOUND CREW 6	jingle bells, drum

Basic Stage Setup

The actors sit on stage in chairs arranged in a semicircle in view of the audience. Costumes and props are stored under the actors' chairs and put on after the opening dance.

The Sound Crew sits with instruments on a table to the right of the stage area, in view of the audience. The tables are set so that the Crew can see the stage.

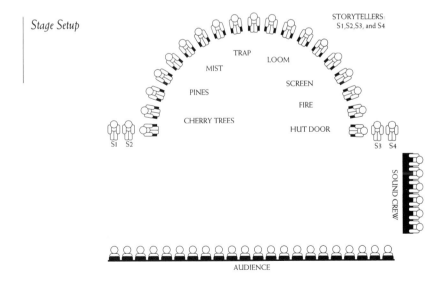

Stage Setup

The play might open with traditional Japanese music, with some performers doing traditional Japanese dance movements. (See Production Notes for music and dance suggestions.) When the dance ends, SOUND CREW 1 fades the music, and SOUND CREW 3 stands dramatically, striking the gong with a flourish to signal the start of the play. STORYTELLER 1 speaks enthusiastically to capture the audience's attention.

⊠ ≈≈≈ ⊠ ≈≈≈ ⊠ ≈≈≈ ⊠ ≈≈≈ ⊠ ≈≈≈ ⊠ ≈≈≈ ⊠

Scene One

Characters Storytellers, Old Man, Old Woman, Peaked Hut Roof, Hearth, Fire, Pines, Swirling Snow

STORYTELLER 1: The story of The Crane Maiden.

(SOUND CREW 3 *strikes gong.*)

STORYTELLER 2: A folk tale from Japan.

(SOUND CREW 3 *strikes gong.*)

STORYTELLER 3: Mukashi, mukashi, or long, long ago, there was a poor old man and woman.

(SOUND CREW 4 *strikes wood block to accompany couple walking to center stage.*)

STORYTELLER 4: They lived in a hut deep in the forest.

(SOUND CREW 6 *rings jingle bells as two* PEAKED HUT ROOF *actors form a roof and couple enters.* PEAKED HUT ROOF *sits.*)

STORYTELLER 1: They had little but were grateful for what they had.

STORYTELLER 2: Every morning they bowed to the East to show gratitude for the life they had.

(SOUND CREW 1 *strikes high piano note three times as couple bows ritualistically to East.*)

STORYTELLER 3: They went to the hearth.

(SOUND CREW 4 *strikes wood block as couple walks to* HEARTH *that forms upstage center with* FIRE *behind it.* FIRE *keeps fire prop behind back until the fire is lit.*)

STORYTELLER 4: The old woman lit the flames.

(SOUND CREW 3 *shakes tambourine as* OLD WOMAN *mimes lighting fire and* FIRE *appears, shimmering slowly.*)

STORYTELLER 1: They prayed to the hearth gods to help them live an honorable life.

(OLD MAN *and* OLD WOMAN *clap hands twice as a signal to awaken the gods within, fold hands in prayer, close eyes, and bow heads.*)

STORYTELLER 2: Each day the woman swept the floor so that it was spotless.

(SOUND CREW 1–3 *shake rattles and* SOUND CREW 5 *scrapes sand blocks for floor sweeping as* OLD WOMAN *mimes sweeping.*)

STORYTELLER 3: One freezing winter day the old man put on a harness to gather twigs.

(OLD MAN *mimes putting on heavy harness.*)

STORYTELLER 4: He bowed good fortune to his wife.

Developing Scripts for Myths and Tales

OLD MAN (*bowing*): Good fortune.

(*One note at a time,* SOUND CREW 1 *plays notes F#, G#, A# on middle of piano keyboard or resonator bells after each "good fortune," the good fortune theme.*)

OLD WOMAN: Good fortune.

(SOUND CREW 1 *plays good fortune theme.* OLD WOMAN *bows in return and* OLD MAN *exits but through doorway formed by* PEAKED HUT ROOF *actors.* PEAKED HUT ROOF *sits.*)

STORYTELLER 1: The wind whistled sharply.

(*Actors in chairs move side to side and whistle.*)

STORYTELLER 2: Tall pines blew this way and that.

(SOUND CREW 2 *plays two piano notes in rapid succession as* PINES *form a row upstage, bending from side to side. Actors whistle.*)

STORYTELLER 3: Icy snow swirled.

(SOUND CREW 3 *shakes tambourine as* SWIRLING SNOW *moves around stage and returns to seat.*)

STORYTELLER 4: The old man trudged one foot after another through the snow.

(SOUND CREW 4 *strikes wood block firmly for trudging as* OLD MAN *mimes strenuous walking.*)

STORYTELLER 1: And he sang...

OLD MAN: Good fortune.

(SOUND CREW 1 *plays good fortune theme.*)

OLD MAN: Good fortune.

(SOUND CREW 1 *plays good fortune theme.*)

OLD MAN: Good fortune.

(SOUND CREW 1 *plays good fortune theme.*)

STORYTELLER 2: The pines seemed to echo his words.

PINE 1: Good fortune.

(SOUND CREW 1 *plays good fortune theme.*)

PINE 2: Good fortune.

(SOUND CREW 1 *plays good fortune theme.*)

PINE 3: Good fortune.

(SOUND CREW 1 *plays good fortune theme.*)

STORYTELLER 3: But no twigs were in sight.

⊠ ≋≋ ⊠ ≋≋ ⊠ ≋≋ ⊠ ≋≋ ⊠ ≋≋ ⊠ ≋≋ ⊠

Scene Two

Characters   Storytellers, Mist, Old Man, Crane, Steel Trap, Old Woman, Fire, Swirling Snow.

STORYTELLER 4: Suddenly a mist floated in.

(SOUND CREW 5 *dings triangle lightly three times as* MIST *forms upstage.* MIST *actors extend arms holding mist fabric while kneeling or standing sideways to audience so that they do not obstruct the view of the scene.* CRANE MAIDEN *and* STEEL TRAP *hide behind* MIST.)

STORYTELLER 1: Behind the mist, the old man heard...

STORYTELLER 2: Basabasa, basabasa, basabasa.

(SOUND CREW 4 *rubs sand blocks after each "basabasa."*)

STORYTELLER 3: Behind the mist, a crane flapped her wings. Her leg was caught in the jaws of a steel trap.

(CRANE MAIDEN *and* STEEL TRAP *emerge from behind* MIST. STEEL TRAP *uses arms and body to represent trap.* CRANE MAIDEN *flaps desperately with hurt leg displayed and extended.*)

STORYTELLER 4: The man pried the trap apart.

(SOUND CREW 2 *scrapes guiro three times as* OLD MAN *exerts energy prying open* TRAP. MIST *sits.* STEEL TRAP *sits.*)

STORYTELLER 1: The crane limped out from the trap.

(SOUND CREW 5 *dings triangle for limping.*)

STORYTELLER 2: The man reached to help.

STORYTELLER 3: But the crane pushed off and flew into the air.

(SOUND CREW 5 *dings triangle three times as* CRANE MAIDEN *swoops gracefully around stage.*)

STORYTELLER 4: Four more cranes joined her.

(SOUND CREW 5 *dings triangle as each* CRANE *joins her, one at a time, as she swoops past their seats on the stage.*)

STORYTELLER 1: They circled three times.

(*One note at a time,* SOUND CREW 2 *plays notes F♯, G♯, A♯, C♯, D♯ on piano or resonator bell—the crane theme—as* CRANES *circle the stage three times.*)

STORYTELLER 2: The cranes disappeared.

(SOUND CREW 2 *plays crane theme as they disappear.* CRANES *sit.* CRANE MAIDEN *goes behind curtain or other concealed spot to put on kimono and become maiden.*)

STORYTELLER 3: The old man hurried home.

(SOUND CREW 4 *strikes wood block as* OLD MAN *rushes to hut.* PEAKED HUT ROOF *forms.*)

STORYTELLER 4: By his door, he found twigs that were not there before.

(SOUND CREW 5 *dings triangle.*)

STORYTELLER 1: The man picked them up.

(SOUND CREW 5 *dings triangle three times as* OLD MAN *picks up three twigs.*)

STORYTELLER 2: He hurried inside the hut.

(SOUND CREW 6 *rings jingle bells.* OLD MAN *enters hut.* PEAKED HUT ROOF *sits.*)

STORYTELLER 3: His wife bowed in joy when she saw the sticks.

STORYTELLER 4: The old man told the story of how he found a crane in a trap and set her free.

STORYTELLER 1: The old woman went to the hearth. She put a twig on the fire.

(HEARTH *and* FIRE *form.*)

STORYTELLER 2: The flames danced.

(SOUND CREW 3 *shakes tambourines as* FIRE *dances.* FIRE *and* HEARTH *move to the side and sit motionless.*)

STORYTELLER 3: They prayed for the crane's good fortune.

(SOUND CREW 1 *plays good fortune theme.* OLD WOMAN *and* OLD MAN *bow and freeze in a gesture of prayer.*)

STORYTELLER 4: Suddenly everything was silent.

(EVERYONE *freezes.*)

STORYTELLER 1: Snow hung suspended in the air.

(SWIRLING SNOW *displays snow and stands motionless.*)

STORYTELLER 2: There was a light crunch, crunch, crunch on the hard snow.

(SOUND CREW 2 *scrapes guiro as* CRANE MAIDEN *enters, walking with erect posture, toes slightly inward, head tilted to side for accent, hands up, elbows out.*)

STORYTELLER 3: There was a tapping on the door.

(PEAKED HUT ROOF *forms and* SOUND CREW 4 *taps wood block as* CRANE MAIDEN *mimes knocking on door.*)

Scene Three

Characters Storytellers, Old Man, Old Woman, Crane Maiden, Hearth, Fire, Japanese Screen, Loom

STORYTELLER 4: The man opened the door.

STORYTELLER 1: There was a maiden in a white kimono and red obi.

≋ ≋≋≋≋ ≋ ≋≋≋≋ ≋ ≋≋≋≋ ≋ ≋≋≋≋ ≋ ≋≋≋≋ ≋ ≋≋≋≋ ≋

STORYTELLER 2: She bowed and pointed toward the forest.

CRANE MAIDEN (*bowing head slightly and making a sweeping, wing-like gesture toward the woods*): I've lost my way.

STORYTELLER 3: The old man and woman led her to the hearth.

(HEARTH *and* FIRE *move into position as* OLD MAN *and* OLD WOMAN *move to either side of* CRANE MAIDEN.)

STORYTELLER 4: Red flames swirled gracefully as she knelt by it.

(SOUND CREW 5 *dings triangle as* FIRE *dances and* CRANE MAIDEN *kneels.*)

STORYTELLER 1: The old woman served rice.

STORYTELLER 2: The girl watched the couple closely as she slowly ate each grain.

(SOUND CREW 5 *dings triangle for each grain eaten.* CRANE MAIDEN *mimes eating with chopsticks.*)

STORYTELLER 3: The woman led the maiden to a screen to sleep.

(JAPANESE SCREEN *stands, holding the screen cloth perpendicular to the audience in the open screen position so as not to distract from the following sequence. Cloth is later turned facing the audience in closed position.*)

STORYTELLER 4: Near the screen was a loom.

(SOUND CREW 5 *dings triangle as* LOOM *forms.*)

STORYTELLER 1: The maiden examined the loom.

(SOUND CREW 5 *dings triangle as* CRANE MAIDEN *examines loom carefully.*)

STORYTELLER 2: The maiden closed the screen.

(CRANE MAIDEN *pretends to pull screen to cover the loom.* JAPANESE SCREEN *actors follow her. The cloth now faces the audience.* JAPANESE SCREEN *actors stand sideways to be more inconspicuous.* FIRE *and* HEARTH *sit.*)

STORYTELLER 3: The maiden bowed her head and went behind the screen.

(SOUND CREW 5 *dings triangle as* CRANE MAIDEN *moves behind screen.*)

STORYTELLER 4: The couple sat by the screen.

STORYTELLER 1: Who was their visitor?

STORYTELLER 2: Why had she come?

STORYTELLER 3: At last they fell asleep.

(OLD MAN *and* OLD WOMAN *slowly lie down on either side of the* JAPANESE SCREEN.)

STORYTELLER 4: All night they heard tonkara, tonkara, tonkara, tonkara, as if someone was weaving on the loom.

(SOUND CREW 2 *scrapes guiro to simulate a shuttle moving back and forth on a loom.*)

STORYTELLER 1: The next morning the maiden presented the couple with a beautiful piece of cloth.

(CRANE MAIDEN *steps from behind* SCREEN *and displays an imaginary cloth that she holds in both hands, presenting it to show it off.* SCREEN *returns to sideways, open position.*)

CRANE MAIDEN (*handing couple cloth*): Sell the cloth and you will be poor no longer.

STORYTELLER 2: The couple took the cloth.

(*The couple take corners of the cloth, displaying it the to audience.*)

STORYTELLER 3: They thanked her.

OLD MAN (*bowing, examining cloth*): Thank you.

OLD WOMAN (*bowing*): Thank you, thank you.

STORYTELLER 4: They could not sell the precious cloth.

OLD WOMAN: It is too precious.

OLD MAN: It is too precious.

CRANE MAIDEN (*bowing*): I will make another to sell.

STORYTELLER 1: The maiden stepped to the screen.

STORYTELLER 2: She held up a hand, telling them to promise never to look at her while she was weaving.

CRANE MAIDEN (*holding up her hand in warning*): Promise never to look at me while I weave.

STORYTELLER 3: The couple nodded.

STORYTELLER 4: The screen closed.

(SOUND CREW *5 dings triangle as* JAPANESE SCREEN *conceals* CRANE MAIDEN *and* LOOM. *Behind the screen,* CRANE MAIDEN *removes her kimono and obi and dons crane outfit. She holds a big white feather to weave with.*)

Scene Four

Characters Storytellers, Old Man, Old Woman, Crane Maiden, Swirling Snow, Japanese Screen, Loom, Pines, Fire, Crane, Cherry Tree

STORYTELLER 1: The couple knelt by the screen.

(*Couple kneel with heads tilted and ears near* JAPANESE SCREEN *in a gesture of listening.*)

STORYTELLER 2: Again came tonkara, tonkara, tonkara.

(SOUND CREW *2 scrapes guiro.*)

STORYTELLER 3: Outside the wind whistled.

(*Actors whistle and move from side to side.*)

STORYTELLER 4: The icy snow swirled.

⊠ ≈⊠≈ ⊠ ≈⊠≈ ⊠ ≈⊠≈ ⊠ ≈⊠≈ ⊠ ≈⊠≈ ⊠ ≈⊠≈ ⊠

(SWIRLING SNOW *moves slowly but energetically, reaching up, stooping down, moving all around outside of the hut.*)

STORYTELLER 1: The couple stared at the screen.

STORYTELLER 2: Tonkara, tonkara, tonkara, tonkara.

(SOUND CREW 2 *scrapes guiro.*)

STORYTELLER 3: They wondered and wondered about their visitor.

STORYTELLER 4: Finally they stood.

(SOUND CREW 4 *strikes wood block once emphatically as couple stands.*)

STORYTELLER 1: One peek couldn't hurt.

(*The couple look at each other in consultation.*)

STORYTELLER 2: They crept slowly to the screen.

(SOUND CREW 4 *taps wood block lightly as couple creeps with stealthy, stylized, slow-motion steps to screen.*)

STORYTELLER 3: They peeked through a crack.

(SOUND CREW 5 *dings triangle as couple takes slow, stylized, exaggerated peek over corners of screen.*)

STORYTELLER 4: The screen parted.

(SOUND CREW 5 *dings triangle twice as one* JAPANESE SCREEN *actor drops a corner of cloth. The other actor keeps holding the other corner.*)

STORYTELLER 1: They jumped back. For there was a crane weaving her feathers in the loom.

(*Couple jump back and* CRANE MAIDEN *is revealed weaving with the feather in exaggerated weaving motions, displaying the big white feather.*)

STORYTELLER 2: The Crane Maiden looked at them, startled.

(SOUND CREW 5 *dings triangle as* CRANE MAIDEN *does stylized "mie"* [*see* Production Notes], *turning and staring at them with enlarged eyes.*)

STORYTELLER 3: She stood and froze in alarm.

(SOUND CREW 5 *dings triangle as* CRANE MAIDEN *does grander mie, raising wings in gesture of alarm toward the audience, continuing to stare and displaying her heightened emotional state.*)

STORYTELLER 4: She dropped a feather and flew to the door.

(SOUND CREW 5 *dings triangle several times as* CRANE MAIDEN *tosses feather in sweeping gesture and flies to door.*)

STORYTELLER 1: The door swung open.

(SOUND CREW 6 *rings jingle bells for door opening.*)

STORYTELLER 2: The old woman reached to stop her.

(SOUND CREW 5 *dings triangle as* OLD WOMAN *does stylized reaching gesture and freezes.*)

STORYTELLER 3: The Crane Maiden hopped away.

(SOUND CREW 5 *dings triangle.*)

STORYTELLER 4: She raised a wing to the woman and said...

CRANE MAIDEN (*arm raised*): I was the crane your husband saved. Now that you have seen me in my true form, I must leave you.

STORYTELLER 1: She pushed off and disappeared into the distance.

(SOUND CREW 2 *plays crane theme as* CRANE MAIDEN *flies off.*)

STORYTELLER 2: Many days passed.

STORYTELLER 3: The couple often knelt by the fire thinking about their crane daughter.

(COUPLE *return to* HEARTH *and kneel.*)

STORYTELLER 4: One day just at spring the cherry trees bloomed.

(CHERRY TREES *create a beautiful visual display along front of stage.*)

STORYTELLER 1: The couple heard...

STORYTELLER 2: Basabasa, basabasa.

(SOUND CREW 5 *scrapes sand blocks as couple tilt heads as if listening.*)

STORYTELLER 3: Basabasa, basabasa.

(SOUND CREW 5 *scrapes sand blocks.*)

STORYTELLER 4: They looked and saw five cranes in a row flapping their wings.

(SOUND CREW 5 *dings triangle as* CRANES *go in front of* CHERRY TREES *and flap wings.*)

STORYTELLER 1: The cranes circled three times.

(SOUND CREW 2 *plays crane theme for each circling.*)

STORYTELLER 2: All but one flew off.

(SOUND CREW 5 *dings triangle.*)

STORYTELLER 3: She stopped, lifted a wing, and bowed her head.

(SOUND CREW 5 *dings triangle as* CRANE MAIDEN *freezes with upstage wing raised and head bowed.*)

Developing Scripts for Myths and Tales

STORYTELLER 4: The couple knew it was their crane daughter who had not forgotten them after all.

STORYTELLER 1: They, too, lifted their arms. For a moment, nothing moved.

(SOUND CREW 5 *dings triangle as couple freezes with arms lifted, creating a frozen picture.*)

STORYTELLER 2: The crane gently flapped her wings as she turned toward the cherry trees.

(SOUND CREW 2 *plays crane theme as* CRANE MAIDEN *faces* CHERRY TREES.)

STORYTELLER 3: And the cherry trees seemed to bow farewell as the Crane Maiden disappeared behind them.

(SOUND CREW 2 *plays crane theme as she disappears behind the trees.* SOUND CREW 1 *plays taped Japanese music as the dancers repeat stylized movements of the Japanese Crane Dance, performed at the beginning of the play.* SOUND CREW 3 *strikes gong when dance is finished and music has faded.*)

Finale

STORYTELLER 1 (*stepping center and bowing*): Arigato Gozaimasu. Thank you, students, adults, too.

(*Pronounced "ah-ree-GAH-tow go-zah-MAH-soo."* SOUND CREW 3 *strikes gong.*)

STORYTELLER 2 (*bowing*): For watching so kindly our show for you.

STORYTELLER 3: Of a Japanese legend, old yet new.

STORYTELLER 4: We hope it came alive for you.

STORYTELLER 1: And here's a last tip, from us, your friends.

STORYTELLER 2 (*holding up book*): Read a book of these legends from beginning to end.

STORYTELLER 3: And study different cultures wherever they may be.

STORYTELLER 4: For the more that you know, the more you'll be...

(STORYTELLERS *gesture to all performers.*)

EVERYONE (*making big circular gesture around their heads*): Free!

STORYTELLER 1: The actors are...

STORYTELLER 2: The Sound Crew is...

STORYTELLER 3: The Storytellers are...

STORYTELLER 4: Arigato Gozaimasu.

To end the performance, STORYTELLERS 1–4 *introduce the performers, having them stand and say their names loudly and clearly. When all are standing,* STORYTELLERS 1–4 *turn toward them and raise arms. Everyone follows, raising their arms and bringing them down together for a group bow, saying "Arigato Gozaimasu" as they do so. Performers then sit for the audience performance discussion.*

Story Questions and Research Topics

To spark students' interest and enrich the cultural experience, provide a variety of materials for investigation, dramatic play, study, and observation. Suggestions include artifacts, clothing, utensils, photographs, artwork, and books. Discussion questions and research topics can be pursued before embarking on a drama experience, during play rehearsal, or after the production to support the culture being introduced.

Story Questions

1. Even though the old couple are poor with few possessions, they thank the gods every day for what they have. Why do they do that?

2. The couple are honorable. What does it mean to be honorable?

3. Why do you think the story had the crane weave rather than, say, make fancy jewelry for the couple?

4. Why would the couple not sell the beautiful cloth?

5. Why do you think the maiden does not want the couple to watch while she weaves the cloth?

6. Why do you think the couple peeked? Why was it difficult not to peek? Would you have peeked? Explain your answer.

7. Why do you think being seen at the loom caused the Crane Maiden to leave?

8. Why do you think the crane would not or could not transform back into a maiden and stay with the couple after they saw her at the loom?

9. What is the tone of this story? Is it sad or happy or a mixture of both? Explain your answer.

10. The Japanese have a great appreciation for the changing seasons. How is this shown in the play?

11. The story of the Crane Maiden is perhaps Japan's most loved folk legend. Every year thousands of Japanese see some version of the story in a play, movie, or opera, or read a version in a book. Why do you think they enjoy it so much? What do you like best about the story?

Theater-Performance Questions

1. This play uses some conventions of Japanese Kabuki theatre. Kabuki theatre, dating back to the seventeenth century, was started by a woman who performed dance dramas. Kabuki still includes many elements of dance. What is dancelike about the way the actors in this play move?

2. Kabuki plays can have several long acts and take all day to perform. People often bring their lunch and eat as they watch the performance. How does this differ from the way people usually attend the theater in the United States? Would you like to go to a theatrical event that lasted all day? What would be the advantages and disadvantages?

3. The Japanese theatre emphasizes a lot of bright display of objects. Where do you see things displayed theatrically in this play?

4. In Kabuki theatre, things are what they are, but they are often symbolic or mean something else, too. For example, what might be the meaning of the flames dancing higher and turning red when the maiden appears in this play? What is the symbolism of the blooming cherry trees at the end of the play?

5. Kabuki theatre is the "actors' theatre," meaning that the actor is the most important element in the play. Some believe that good acting is the most important element in any play production. What is your opinion? What else is important to make a good production?

6. Japanese audiences particularly like to watch actors perform *mies* (pronounced MEE-ays), expressing extreme emotion with the entire body and then freezing in a pose that displays that emotion. Find places in this play where the characters might make a *mie* to register strong emotion.

7. An important Japanese theatrical convention is the use of Prop People. These actors dress all in black to appear to be invisible, although they often can be seen while they move about on the stage. Why should they appear to be invisible? What is the advantage of having them in a play?

8. Japanese theatre uses musicians on stage to play music and create sound effects. What do such effects add to a play? What is the advantage of having live musicians? What qualities does a good theatre musician need?

9. The two major kinds of theatre in Japan are the Kabuki and Noh Drama. Noh Drama is older than Kabuki, dating from the fourteenth century. It was performed for the wealthy; Kabuki was performed for the middle class. Study both Kabuki and Noh Drama. Bring in pictures showing each. What are their similarities and differences? Why do you think people now need or want Kabuki theatre? Which form of Japanese theatre do you think you would most enjoy seeing? Give reasons for your answer.

Research Topics

1. Animals changing into humans is a common theme in Japanese tales. Find other Japanese stories in which a person becomes an animal. How does the person or animal use its power?

2. Stories from many cultures feature characters that peek at something after they are told not to look. Read one of these stories. What are the consequences of the characters' curiosity? Compare this story to *The Crane Maiden*. How is it similar and how is it different?

3. Japanese screens may be decorative, but they are also used to create different rooms within one room. Why do the Japanese need this device? Where and how have you seen these beautiful screens used in other countries?

4. The Japanese have more festivals than almost any other culture. A favorite is the Cherry Blossom Festival. When is it held? What do families do during this festival? Why is it so important?

5. Japan is a small country with a large population, and it is one of the wealthiest countries in the world. Why is it so successful?

6. Haiku is a form of Japanese poetry that uses seventeen syllables in each poem. What subjects does it treat? Write a haiku poem about the Crane Maiden or one of the four seasons.

7. The crane is revered in Japan and other cultures. Many cultures believed it to be sacred. The Japanese call it *tsuru* (soo-roo), meaning "royal." Its image is used to decorate clothes and fans. People have crane statues in their yards. Study a crane and its movements. What about it may contribute to it being held in such high esteem?

8. The Japanese give nature special attention. What in the play shows this to be the case? What other cultures in this book show a reverence for nature? How does their behavior show this?

9. Shinto is the oldest Japanese religion. According to Shintoism, gods and goddesses live inside of rocks, trees, plants, waterfalls, animals, and the human heart. What other cultures represented in this book believe that gods and goddesses dwell inside of things?

10. Another main religion of Japan is Buddhism, which came from Korea and China in the sixth century. Buddhists believe that people are born over and over again, and all their actions in this life effect their next lives. Zen Buddhism, the form practiced by the Japanese, emphasizes meditating to become wise. What other religions share similar beliefs? In what ways are they similar? In what ways are they different? What is the value of meditation?

Selected Bibliography
Versions of "The Crane Maiden"

Bang, Molly. *Dawn*. New York: William Morrow and Company, 1983. A modern picture book version of "The Crane Maiden," set in Canada and featuring a Canadian Goose.

Matsutani, Miyoki. *The Crane Maiden*. Illustrated by Chihro Twaski. New York: Parents Magazine Press, 1968. An enjoyable version of the story, appealing to grades three and four. This book is out of print, but may be available at a library.

Yagawa, Sumiko. *The Crane Wife*. Illustrated by Suekichi Akaba. New York: William Morrow and Company, 1981. Excellent retelling of "The Crane Maiden," with illustrations capturing Japan and its culture.

Plays and Stories

Bang, Molly. *The Paper Crane*. New York: Greenwillow, 1985. Modern retelling of an ancient folk tale of a restaurant-owner who feeds a penniless stranger and is rewarded by a magical paper crane. Illustrated with intriguing paper cut-outs.

Goodman, Robert B., and Robert A. Spicer. *Urashimo Taro*. Illustrated by George Suyeoka. Hawaii: Island Heritage, 1973. A lavishly illustrated story of a young man and his adventures under the sea.

Mosel, Arlene. *The Funny Little Woman*. Illustrated by Blair Lent. New York: Dutton, 1972. Winner of the Caldecott medal; delightful and excellent to dramatize.

O'Toole, Maureen A. *Ama and the White Crane.* New Orleans, LA: Anchorage Press, 1978. A moving and charming Kabuki-style play for older students.

Pratt, Davis, and Elsa Kula. *Magic Animals of Japan.* Berkeley, CA: Parnassus Press, 1967. Describes symbolism of the crane and eleven other animals in Japanese culture. Includes a version of "The Crane Maiden." The short tales of animals are good to dramatize.

Quayle, Eric. *The Shining Princess and Other Japanese Legends.* Illustrated by Michael Forman. New York: Arcade Publishing, 1989. Ten tales, beautifully illustrated.

Sakade, Florence, ed. *Japanese Children's Favorite Stories.* Illustrated by Yoshisuke Kurosa. Rutland, VT: Charles E. Tuttle, 1988. Traditional stories loved by Japanese children, including "Peach Boy," "The Tongue-Cut Sparrow," and "The Rabbit in the Moon."

Swortzell, Lowell, and Nancy Swortzell. *Cinderella, The World's Favorite Fairy Tale.* Charlottesville, VA: New Plays Incorporated, 1993. Versions of Cinderella from Native America, Russia, and China with clearly described acting activities. Includes a multicultural study guide.

Tseng Jeau, and Maou-Sien. *Three Strong Woman: A Tale from Japan.* New York: Viking, 1990. When the famous wrestler Forever Mountain tickles a plump little girl, his punishment is to be trained by her, her mother, and her grandmother. Amusing and enjoyable to act.

Social Studies

Downer, Lesley. *Countries of the World—Japan.* New York: Bookwright Press, 1990. An insightful account of modern-day Japan.

Kaufman, Bobbie. *Japan, the Culture.* New York: Crabtree Publishing, 1989. Excellent overview and striking photos of the Japanese people, their environment, and their culture.

Shelley, Rex. *Cultures of the World: Japan.* New York: Marshall Cavendish, 1990. Well-researched and informative.

Tames, Richard. Japan: *The Land and Its People.* Morristown, NJ: Silver Burdett Press, 1975. Informative, succinct, beautifully illustrated.

Performance

Scott, A. C. *The Kabuki Theatre of Japan.* New York: Macmillan, Inc., 1966. A clear and in-depth study of the art of the Kabuki theatre, aimed at high school students and adults.

Other Books

Owens, Mary Beth. *Counting Cranes.* Boston: Little, Brown, 1994. Splendid book showing images of cranes and describing their migration.

Roop, Peter, and Connie Roop. *Seasons of the Cranes.* New York: Walker and Company, 1989. Beautiful color pictures follow the red-crested whooping crane through the seasons. A helpful resource for enacting the crane.

CHAPTER NINE

Jack and the Beanstalk
A Traditional Folk Tale of Magic and its Earth-Shaking Consequences

This folk tale has been known in Britain since 1734, where it was first published as The Story of Jack Spriggin and the Enchanted Bean. *The story features a boy who overcomes a giant. The theme of a youthful hero overcoming a giant or other ogre is common in British and other European fairy stories. This story continues to be a favorite today, and new versions appear in books and plays every year.*

The story begins when Jack and his mother decide to sell their cow. Jack trades the cow for magic beans which grow into a huge beanstalk. Jack climbs the stalk through the clouds to a magical place where he discovers the home of a Giant. The Giant's Wife feeds Jack and conceals him from the greedy Giant. Jack observes the Giant counting huge stacks of gold and, when the Giant tires and falls asleep, Jack nimbly steals some gold and races home. On a second trip up the beanstalk, Jack discovers the Giant's special hen who lays golden eggs. Again, when the Giant falls asleep, Jack steals the Hen and races home. On a third trip up the beanstalk, Jack sees the Giant's golden harp. This time, when Jack tries to steal the harp, the Giant awakens and chases Jack down the beanstalk. Jack races to the bottom and chops down the beanstalk. The Giant falls down through the air and plummets deep into the earth, leaving Jack and his mother to enjoy their lives with the magical hen and singing harp.

Acting Exercises

The following acting exercises may be used to help students practice acting principles and develop the characters that make up the cast of this play.

Role-Playing Jack and the Giant

Goal To pantomime actions of the characters to develop characterization and experience their feelings.

Acting Principle Belief.

Procedure Describe the following situations and have the whole class depict the actions of each character.

- You are Jack. You are very hungry because you had no supper. The Giant's Wife has put before you a big loaf of crusty French bread on a plate. You see the bread and pick it up. Rip into it with your teeth and chew it quickly. Now pick up a frosty, cold glass of milk. Drink a big gulp to help swallow the dry bread. Pick up the bread for another bite. Freeze. The Giant is coming.

- You are the Giant. You love money. Pick up a huge bag of gold coins. Feel the weight. Turn the bag upside down and pour the gold all over the table. Listen to it clink. Pick up a big coin and bite into it to confirm its value. Stack up the big gold pieces in piles, lovingly examining each coin. Feel your eyes get heavy as you become drowsy. Nod off to sleep and snore loudly. Freeze in a stupor.

Role-Playing the Beanstalk

Goal To act out the growth of a beanstalk.

Acting Principles Belief, Control.

Optional Materials Strike a triangle or ring a small bell on each count of the beanstalk's growth and then continually when the magical beanstalk garden forms.

Procedure Guide students through the stages of becoming a beanstalk, beginning with planting the seeds and ending with Jack climbing the stalk. Once the beanstalks are formed, pluck off and taste a few of the magical beans, commenting to students on their delicious taste.

- You are Jack. You open your hand and see three bright blue, shiny, magical beans. You want to plant them. You kneel on the ground and dig a deep hole. You put the beans in and cover them with earth. Pat the cool, brown earth down on all sides. Water the beans well. Finally, use your hands to create warm sun rays shining down to help the seeds grow.

- You are a bean seed. Make yourself small and huddle tight under the earth. Feel the rain fall gently on you and the sun send its warm beams all over you. On a count of eight, you will slowly grow up into a beanstalk until you are fully extended as a tall magical beanstalk.

- You are a beanstalk. Sway slowly in the moonlight. As morning comes, you slowly fade back to earth on a count of eight until you are completely still.

- You are Jack. You awake and see a magical beanstalk from your bed. Get up. Go to the window. Look at how the beanstalk reaches up into the sky. Climb out the window. Bend down low and get on the lowest branches. Slowly climb up the stalk, branch by branch. Look around. What is up there?

Role-Playing the Giant

Goal To run in controlled slow motion.

Acting Principle Control.

Procedure Explain that it is necessary for the Giant to look as if he is frantically chasing Jack, but there is not enough room on the stage for an actual chase. Thus, the Giant must pretend that thick clouds are stopping him as he desperately runs. You may wish to divide the class into two groups, so that one can observe as the other acts out the scene.

- You are the Giant. You want to catch Jack because he has stolen your money, hen, and harp. Take a desperate running stance. Run in place and push with all your might to get through the heavy clouds. The clouds are so thick that you can hardly pick your legs up. Freeze, using your whole face and body to show how thick and heavy the clouds are.

Circle Walk Character Transformation

Goal To use voice and movement to express each character.

Acting Principles Belief, Voice and Movement.

Materials Use a drum to create a beat and pitch that matches the pace and style of each character, tapping lightly and quickly for characters such as the hen and heavier and more slowly for the cow and Giant.

Procedure Students form a circle and begin walking to the beat of a drum. Give the following directions while beating the drum. Students transform from one character to another as they walk in a circle, saying the appropriate tag dialogue.

- You are yourself, walking to the beat of the drum.
- You are Jack's energetic mother, wringing her hands, worried because you have no money. Freeze. "I'm so worried, Jack."
- You are happy-go-lucky Jack, skipping because you feel you can conquer anything. Freeze. "Don't worry, Mother."
- You are the heavy cow, taking up a lot of space. You have huge, wide-open eyes and are lumbering close to the earth. Freeze. "Moo."
- You are a 110-year-old man, bent over because your back hurts and your body quivers. Freeze. "How about these beans?"
- You are the Giant's Wife, nervous and fidgeting because your husband is a brute who is always bullying you. Freeze. "Go away, boy."
- You are the heavy Giant, who occupies lots of space and takes big, wide, thumping steps because you like to boss and dominate people. Freeze. "Fee, Fi, Fo, Fum."

- You are the magical hen. Your feet point out because you have big claws. Cluck and flap proudly. Freeze. Cackle and lay a big golden egg.
- You are the dramatic and beautiful golden harp. Move around the circle, showing off your strings and your beauty. Freeze. Sing, "Master, Master."

Speaking as the Characters

Goal To respond to situations as a character would, imitating personality, style, and voice to create dialogue.

Acting Principles Voice and Movement, Control.

Procedure Tell students that they are going to show each characters' feelings in the following scenes and make up something the characters might say in response to the situation. For the first scene, have students brainstorm together what they might say and do for each character. For each subsequent scene, preliminary brainstorming is not necessary.

- You are Jack's mother. The cow gives no milk. Freeze. Speak.
- You are the old man, trying to entice Jack to take the beans. Freeze. Speak.
- You are Jack, seeing the beanstalk for first time. Freeze. Speak.
- You are the Giant's Wife, hearing the Giant come home. Freeze. Speak.
- You are the Giant. You suspect that your wife is not telling the truth about no one being in the house. Freeze. Speak.
- You are the Giant's Wife, trying to convince Giant that no one is in the house. Freeze. Speak.
- You are the Giant, discovering that the gold is gone. Freeze. Speak.
- You are Jack's mother when she sees the gold. Freeze. Speak.

Production Notes

The following guidelines may be used to enhance the quality of the production with dance movements and simple costumes.

English Wake-Up the Spring Dance

Music "Bean Setting," "Princess Royal," "Greensleeves," or "Young Collins" from the audio tape entitled *Morris On.* Available from Carthage Records, 100 Jersey Avenue, New Brunswick, NJ, 08901. Any up-tempo English folk music with bells and fiddles is suitable; lively hammered dulcimer music works well.

Purpose and Style Light, joyous movements awaken spring and drive Old Man Winter away.

Materials A wreath of flowers to form a headpiece or ceremonial paper hats decorated with flowers or ribbons. (See *Costume Suggestions.*) Dancers might wave ribbons or lightly shake tambourines or bells as they dance.

Formation A circle moving in a clockwise direction.

Steps and Stances Arm movements are flowing, calling on spirits to welcome the green earth. Knees are raised high, and stomping is clear and emphatic.

   Step One: The leader stands upstage center with hands raised, holding jingle bells in one hand and waiting for music to begin. When the music begins, the leader lightly rings bells and skips down center, raising arms together in flowing, circular movements.

Step One

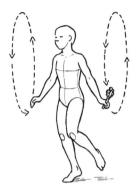

Facing the audience, the leader skips backward to the starting position, lowering arms. The action is repeated twice, ending downstage.

Step Two: The leader skips in place in a circle, ringing bells above the head. The action is repeated. The leader then freezes and holds bells up, signaling the performers to rise from their seats.

Step Two

Step Three: Performers rise and form a circle with the leader raising hands above their heads to show that they are ready to begin.

Step Four: When all are ready, the leader skips in and out of the circle twice, raising and lowering both arms at the same time and ringing bells. The other dancers follow.

Step Five: The leader turns clockwise. Everyone skips clockwise in a circle, knees high, circling twice.

Step Six: Upon reaching the starting position, the leader skips into and out from the center of the circle, and the others follow. The action is repeated.

Step Seven: The leader stops, claps hands twice assertively, and puts hands on hips. The dancers do the same. The leader stamps four times to awaken the earth. The other dancers follow the action. To end the dance, the leader turns clockwise and all skip in a circle, knees raised high, and return to their seats. Music fades completely when the last dancer sits.

Step Seven

Finale: The final dance at the conclusion of the play is the same as the opening dance.

Costume Suggestions

For narrative mime presentations, all students wear black clothing—black shirts and black pants—with individual character costumes worn as additional pieces to the all-black attire.

Storyteller One (for Prologue)   Ceremonial paper bag hat with flowers or ribbons.

Storytellers   Tunics, each in a different bright color.

Jack   Peter-Pan style green hat with red feather, brightly colored vest.

Mother   Mob cap (maybe a shower cap or cap used for covering curlers), apron.

Cow   Black, white, or brown fur hat with cow horns attached.

Old Man   Floppy, felt hat such as a deerstalker, with brim turned down.

Giant's Wife   Bonnet, crocheted shawl, apron.

Giant   Wig made from a rag mop or a big furry hat; piece of black fur material draped around shoulders and pinned to create bulk.

Well   No costume other than black clothing is necessary. Arms are held in open, rounded position to resemble the opening of a well.

Oven   No costume other than black clothing is necessary. Actors kneel, facing each other; arms are held out stiffly, parallel to floor, forming the oven door.

Table   No costume other than black clothing is necessary. Actors kneel and use either their arms or their backs to form the tabletop.

Berry Bush   Purple, blue, or red gloves.

Box with Gold   Gold or yellow gloves.

Broom Closet   No costume other than black clothing is necessary. Arms are held erect to indicate closet door.

Hen   Headband with lots of bright red or orange feathers attached. A yellow visor can be worn to form a beak.

Harp   Gold nylon netting draped around shoulders, gold headband or yellow headpiece with gold glitter on it.

Beanstalk   Green no-sew tunics.

Door to Giant's House   No costume other than black clothing is necessary. Actors face each other, holding arms out stiffly and parallel to floor to indicate an entryway.

Clouds   Several yards of white nylon netting.

Earth   A gray or brown cloth big enough to cover the Giant.

Jack and the Beanstalk

A Traditional Folk Tale of Magic
and Its Earth-Shaking Consequences

Cast

FOUR STORYTELLERS (clear, strong, enthusiastic voices and gestures)

JACK (cheerful)

MOTHER (a worrier)

COW (relaxed)

OLD MAN (110 years old)

GIANT'S WIFE (nervous, anxious to please)

GIANT (a bully)

WELL (2)

OVEN (2)

TABLE (2)

BERRY BUSHES (2)

BROOM CLOSET (2)

HEN (likes to cackle)

HARP (very dramatic poses, like a modern dancer)

BEANSTALK (4)

BOX WITH GOLD

DOOR TO GIANT'S HOUSE (2)

CLOUDS (2)

EARTH THAT COVERS GIANT (2)

HOUSE CHORUS (all actors raise their hands and shake their bodies when the Giant enters)

GIANT CHORUS (all actors say "Fee, Fi, Fo, Fum" along with the Giant)

Sound Crew

The Sound Crew is assigned the following instruments to play. Other instruments might be substituted or made with found objects. (See Setting the Scene, Chapter Two, for suggestions.)

SOUND CREW 1   taped dance music, triangle, rattle, wind chimes
SOUND CREW 2   wood block, rattle, small hand bell
SOUND CREW 3   cow bell, tambourine, rattle
SOUND CREW 4   small hand bell, guiro, rattle
SOUND CREW 5   rattle, bass drum
SOUND CREW 6   piano or resonator bells (does not need to know how to play the piano), jingle bells

Basic Stage Setup

The actors sit on stage in chairs arranged in a semicircle in view of the audience. Costumes and props are stored under the actors' chairs and put on after the opening dance. The Sound Crew sits with instruments on a table to the right of the stage area, in view of the audience. The tables are set so that the Crew can see the stage. Stage left is Jack's House. Downstage is the road to the market and the route to the Giant's house. Stage right is the locale of the Giant's House. You may wish to use masking tape to mark where the inanimate objects belong.

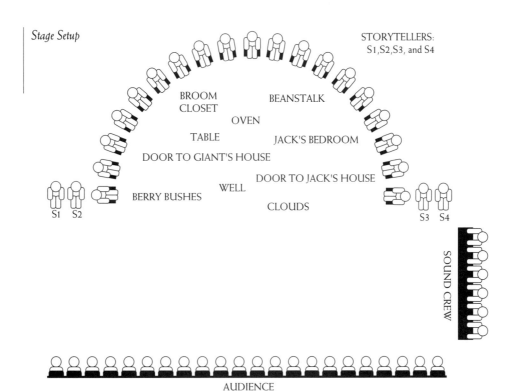

Stage Setup

STORYTELLERS:
S1,S2,S3, and S4

BROOM CLOSET
BEANSTALK
OVEN
TABLE
JACK'S BEDROOM
DOOR TO GIANT'S HOUSE
DOOR TO JACK'S HOUSE
WELL
BERRY BUSHES
CLOUDS
S1 S2
S3 S4
SOUND CREW
AUDIENCE

SOUND CREW 6 *rings jingle bells with a flourish as* STORYTELLER 1 *steps center and speaks in an exciting, dramatic manner, embellishing the speech with dramatic gestures to illustrate it.*

Scene One

Characters   Storytellers, Mother, Jack, Cow

STORYTELLER 1 (*gesturing to stage to begin Prologue*):

This play takes place in England's merry land,

A place of theatre, old and grand.

It has a harp and a hen that squawks.

I bet you've guessed it's Jack and the Beanstalk.

Now to help our play begin,

To make it whirl and make it spin,

We'll do an English springtime dance.

Watch us leap and watch us prance.

> STORYTELLER 1 *gestures toward dancers with a sweeping bow and sits. Lead dancer steps center with jingle bells raised, waiting for taped music to begin.* SOUND CREW 1 *plays taped music and leader begins the dance. (See* Production Notes *for music and dance suggestions.) When dancers sit,* STORYTELLER 1 *begins speaking in a clear, bright voice to grab the audience's attention.*

STORYTELLER 1: The story of Jack and the Beanstalk.

STORYTELLER 2: A tale from merry old England.

STORYTELLER 3: There was once a poor widow.

(SOUND CREW 2 *taps wood block as* MOTHER *walks down center and curtsies.*)

STORYTELLER 4: She had an only son named Jack.

(SOUND CREW 2 *taps wood block as* JACK *skips next to* MOTHER *and bows.*)

STORYTELLER 1: And a cow named Milk-White.

(SOUND CREW 3 *strikes cow bell as* COW *lumbers between* JACK *and* MOTHER.)

STORYTELLER 2: But one morning Milk-White had no milk.

(SOUND CREW 3 *strikes cow bell.*)

COW (*to audience, shaking head no*): Moo.

STORYTELLER 3: Jack's mother was worried.

MOTHER (*wringing hands*): I'm worried. What can we do? What can we do?

STORYTELLER 4: Jack told his mother to leave it to him.

JACK: Leave it to me, Mother. I'll take old Milk-White to market and sell her.

Scene Two

Characters Storytellers, Jack, Cow, Old Man

STORYTELLER 1: So Jack grabbed the cow's halter and skipped off.

   (SOUND CREW 2 *taps wood block for skipping.*)

STORYTELLER 2: The cow mooed.

COW: Moo.

   (SOUND CREW 3 *strikes cow bell after "Moo."*)

STORYTELLER 3: Soon Jack met an old, old man who put up a hand, stopping him.

OLD MAN (*hand held out, body bent over, quavering voice*): Where are you off to, my boy?

JACK (*hands on hips*): I'm off to market to sell our cow.

STORYTELLER 4: The man examined the cow from all sides.

STORYTELLER 1: He reached deep into his pocket.

OLD MAN (*reaching into pocket and opening hand with three imaginary beans*): How about magic beans for your cow?

   (SOUND CREW 2 *and* SOUND CREW 4 *ring bells at mention of magic beans.*)

JACK (*enthusiastically*): Magic beans!

   (SOUND CREW 2 *and* SOUND CREW 4 *ring small hand bells.*)

OLD MAN (*nodding wisely*): Yes, magic. Plant them at night and by morning, they'll grow up through the clouds.

JACK (*peering at beans suspiciously*): Really?

OLD MAN (*nodding*): Yes, really.

STORYTELLER 2: Jack decided to do it.

JACK (*looking at beans again, then up at sky*): I'll do it.

   (SOUND CREW 2 *and* SOUND CREW 4 *ring small hand bells as* JACK *takes magic beans and hands the cow's halter to the* OLD MAN.)

STORYTELLER 3: The man stared at him hard, wishing him good luck.

OLD MAN (*peering at him and tipping hat*): Good luck.

STORYTELLER 4: The old man nodded and went off. The cow mooed happily.

COW (*happily*): Moo.

   (SOUND CREW 3 *strikes cow bell as* COW *happily goes off with* OLD MAN. OLD MAN *and* COW *sit.*)

Scene Three

Characters Storytellers, Jack, Mother, Beanstalk, Clouds

STORYTELLER 1: Jack skipped home.

(SOUND CREW 2 *strikes wood block for skipping.*)

STORYTELLER 2: His mother wondered how much he earned by selling the cow.

MOTHER (*excitedly*): How much did you sell her for?

JACK (*proudly showing beans*): What do you think of these beans?

(SOUND CREW 2 *and* SOUND CREW 4 *ring small hand bells.*)

MOTHER (*eyes enlarging, to audience*): Beans!

(SOUND CREW 2 *and* SOUND CREW 4 *ring small hand bells.*)

JACK (*miming planting*): You plant them at night and by the morning...

MOTHER (*pointing finger at* JACK, *eyes flashing angrily*): You sold our cow for beans!

(SOUND CREW 2 *and* SOUND CREW 4 *ring small hand bells.*)

STORYTELLER 3: Jack's mother tossed the beans out the window.

MOTHER: Out they go.

(SOUND CREW 2 *strikes wood block as beans are thrown out.*)

STORYTELLER 4: Mother sent Jack to bed with no supper.

MOTHER (*pointing to bedroom*): Go to bed.

STORYTELLER 1: Downhearted, Jack went to bed.

(SOUND CREW 2 *strikes wood block slowly as* JACK *walks downheartedly and lies down.*)

STORYTELLER 2: Sleep was restless.

(SOUND CREW 6 *strikes two high piano notes in rapid succession for restlessness as* JACK *twists in sleep. Notes are repeated, as necessary.*)

STORYTELLER 3: That night a beanstalk grew.

(SOUND CREW 1 *slowly dings triangle five times as* BEANSTALK *actors take places, starting as seeds and growing slowly; by fifth ring, stalk is fully grown with arms extended.*)

STORYTELLER 4: The next morning Jack awoke.

(JACK *rises, stretching and squinting at morning sun.*)

STORYTELLER 1: He leaped up and looked out.

(JACK *springs out of bed and races out the door.*)

STORYTELLER 2: The beans had sprung up into a tall beanstalk that swayed in the breeze.

(SOUND CREW 2 *and* SOUND CREW 4 *ring small hand bells several times as* BEANSTALK *sways.*)

Developing Scripts for Myths and Tales

STORYTELLER 3: Jack jumped onto the beanstalk and up he climbed to the sky.

(SOUND CREW 6 *strikes piano notes from lower to higher as* JACK *climbs.*)

STORYTELLER 4: First he hopped among the clouds.

(CLOUD *actors quickly rise and hold out cloud fabric.* SOUND CREW 1 *rings wind chimes and* SOUND CREW 2 *and* SOUND CREW 4 *ring small hand bells as* JACK *lightly hops behind* CLOUD *actors.*)

STORYTELLER 1: Next he walked on a dusty road.

(SOUND CREW 1–5 *shake rattles for walking.* CLOUDS *sit.*)

Scene Four

Characters Storytellers, Jack, Door to Giant's House, Well, Giant's Wife

STORYTELLER 2: He came to a house with a huge door.

(DOOR TO GIANT'S HOUSE *actors take their places and freeze.*)

STORYTELLER 3: A nervous woman was drawing water from a well.

(WELL *actors take their places, kneeling on floor and facing each other with arms open in rounded position.* SOUND CREW 4 *scrapes guiro vigorously as* GIANT'S WIFE *draws water.*)

STORYTELLER 4: She jumped in alarm when she saw Jack.

(SOUND CREW 3 *shakes tambourine as* GIANT'S WIFE *jumps back, surprised.*)

STORYTELLER 1: Jack said, "Good morning," and asked for breakfast.

JACK: Good morning. Please give me some breakfast.

STORYTELLER 2: The woman shooed him to go away.

GIANT'S WIFE (*gesturing with arms*): Go away. My husband is a Giant, and he eats anything alive for breakfast.

JACK (*on hands and knees*): Please. I'm starving.

STORYTELLER 3: Jack looked so pitiful that the Giant's Wife led him to the table.

(*Both enter kitchen through* DOOR. DOOR *remains in place.* TABLE *forms and* JACK *sits behind it.*)

STORYTELLER 4: She brought bread and milk.

(GIANT'S WIFE *mimes carrying small tray;* JACK *mimes eating bread hungrily and gulping milk thirstily.*)

Scene Five

Characters Storytellers, Jack, Giant's Wife, Giant, Oven, Table, Box with Gold

STORYTELLER 1: Jack was pouring more milk when there was a huge thump, thump, thump, thump.

(SOUND CREW 5 *strikes bass drum emphatically for each thump as* JACK *freezes, wide-eyed, and mimes holding pitcher in midair.* GIANT *stands with back to audience, taking wide, in-place thumping steps along with the beating drum.*)

STORYTELLER 2: The whole house began to shake and tremble with the sound of something coming.

(SOUND CREW 3 *shakes tambourine emphatically and* SOUND CREW 1–5 *shake rattles emphatically as* HOUSE CHORUS *raises hands to their heads and shakes whole bodies.*)

GIANT'S WIFE (*hands on head*): It's him!

STORYTELLER 3: She pointed at the oven.

(SOUND CREW 1 *dings triangle as* OVEN *forms.*)

GIANT'S WIFE (*gesturing to oven*): Jump in the oven.

(SOUND CREW 2 *strikes wood block once as* JACK *opens the oven door and again when the door closes.*)

STORYTELLER 4: There was a stronger thump, thump, thump.

(SOUND CREW 5 *strikes drum more emphatically.*)

STORYTELLER 1: The giant stomped into the kitchen.

STORYTELLER 2: He was a big one and he said...

GIANT *and* GIANT CHORUS (*booming, stomping feet, and sniffing*): Fee, Fi, Fo, Fum. I smell the blood of an Englishman. Be he alive, or be he dead, I'll grind his bones to make my bread.

(SOUND CREW 5 *strikes drum after "Fee, Fi, Fo, Fum;"* GIANT *makes grinding motion with hands and* SOUND CREW 4 *scrapes guiro after "grind."*)

STORYTELLER 3: His wife said it was his imagination.

GIANT'S WIFE (*fidgeting*): It's only your imagination.

STORYTELLER 4: She hurried him to the washroom.

GIANT'S WIFE: Go wash up and I'll serve breakfast.

STORYTELLER 1: The Giant growled.

GIANT *and* GIANT CHORUS (*fiercely, showing fists*): Grrr!

STORYTELLER 2: He stomped to the washroom.

(SOUND CREW 5 *strikes drum for stomping.* GIANT *turns his back to the audience and mimes washing hands.*)

STORYTELLER 3: Jack began to crawl out of the oven, but the wife pushed him back in.

GIANT'S WIFE (*finger to lips*): Shhh. Wait until he takes a nap.

STORYTELLER 4: The Giant stomped back and pounded his fist for breakfast.

(SOUND CREW 5 *strikes drum for stomping.* TABLE *takes its place.* GIANT *sits at table, and mimes pounding fist on its surface as* SOUND CREW 5 *strikes drum one last time for pounding fist.*)

GIANT: Wife, bring my breakfast.

STORYTELLER 1: His wife rushed in with four chickens and a pitcher of milk.

(GIANT'S WIFE *rushes around kitchen in a flurry, back and forth from* TABLE.)

STORYTELLER 2: He devoured each chicken and wiped his mouth with his sleeve.

GIANT (*eating one chicken after another, slurping*): One, two, three, four.

STORYTELLER 3: He drank the pitcher of milk in one glug.

GIANT (*raising pitcher and drinking*): Glug!

STORYTELLER 4: He tore open a box and grabbed two bags of gold.

(BOX *forms, and* GIANT *mimes throwing open box cover and greedily grabbing bags of gold.*)

STORYTELLER 1: He poured one bag onto the table.

(SOUND CREW 2 *and* SOUND CREW 4 *ring small hand bells for pouring gold.*)

STORYTELLER 2: The Giant greedily counted his gold coins.

GIANT (*greedily, stacking the gold*): One, two, three, four.

(SOUND CREW 1 *dings triangle for each gold piece counted.*)

STORYTELLER 3: Soon the Giant grew tired, his head nodded, and he fell to the floor, snoring in a stupor.

(SOUND CREW 5 *strikes drum as* GIANT *falls to floor.* SOUND CREW 4 *scrapes guiro for snoring.*)

STORYTELLER 4: The whole house began to shake and tremble with the huge noise.

(HOUSE CHORUS *raises hands to heads, shaking and trembling;* SOUND CREW 3 *shakes tambourine and* SOUND CREW 1–5 *shake rattles as* HOUSE CHORUS *shakes and trembles.*)

STORYTELLER 1: Jack cautiously opened the oven door.

(SOUND CREW 4 *scrapes guiro for squeaky door.* JACK *peeks head out from* OVEN.)

STORYTELLER 2: He tiptoed to the table, took a bag of gold and ran off with it.

(SOUND CREW 2 *strikes wood block for tiptoeing and running.* JACK *exits through* DOOR. DOOR *and* TABLE *then sit in place.*)

Scene Six

Characters Storytellers, Jack, Beanstalk, Clouds, Mother

STORYTELLER 3: Jack came to the beanstalk. He tossed the bag down through the clouds.

Developing Scripts for Myths and Tales

(BEANSTALK *forms.* CLOUDS *take position.* SOUND CREW 2 *strikes wood block emphatically as bag drops.*)

STORYTELLER 4: And he climbed down after it.

(SOUND CREW 6 *strikes piano keys from high to low as* JACK *climbs down.* BEANSTALK *and* CLOUDS *sit.*)

STORYTELLER 1: Jack's mother was thrilled and held up the bag in triumph.

MOTHER (holding bag high in air): I'm thrilled.

(MOTHER *pats* JACK *on back, congratulating him.*)

STORYTELLER 2: They lived on the gold for quite a while.

(SOUND CREW 1 *dings triangle as* JACK *and* MOTHER *together hold up imaginary bag of gold; they admire it and freeze.*)

STORYTELLER 3: But one day the gold ran out.

(JACK *and* MOTHER *drop arms to sides and shake heads sadly.*)

STORYTELLER 4: The next morning, Jack got up early and climbed up the beanstalk.

(BEANSTALK *takes place.* SOUND CREW 6 *strikes piano keys from low to high as* JACK *climbs.*)

STORYTELLER 1: Again he hopped the clouds.

(CLOUDS *take position.* SOUND CREW 1 *rings wind chimes and* SOUND CREW 2 *and* SOUND CREW 4 *ring small hand bells as* JACK *hops behind* CLOUDS.)

STORYTELLER 2: Again he walked the gravel road.

(SOUND CREW 1–5 *shake rattles lightly as* JACK *walks.* CLOUDS *and* BEANSTALK *sit in place.*)

Scene Seven

Characters   Storytellers, Jack, Door to Giant's House, Giant's Wife, Giant, Oven, Table, Hen

STORYTELLER 1: He arrived at the door of the Giant's house.

(DOOR *takes its place and* JACK *enters.*)

STORYTELLER 2: The Giant's Wife, however, was suspicious.

STORYTELLER 3: But Jack begged for breakfast.

JACK (*on hands and knees*): Please, Mum, just a little breakfast.

STORYTELLER 4: The Giant's Wife shook her head no, but Jack looked like he would cry, so she gave in.

STORYTELLER 1: She led him to the table.

(TABLE *forms as* GIANT'S WIFE *directs* JACK *to sit.*)

STORYTELLER 2: She served bread and milk.

STORYTELLER 3: She said to eat quickly and leave.

GIANT'S WIFE (*putting dishes on table*): Eat and leave.

STORYTELLER 4: But immediately there was a thump, thump, thump.

(SOUND CREW 5 *strikes bass drum emphatically with each "thump." GIANT, again with back to audience, stomps in place with wide steps. After several thumps, SOUND CREW 3 shakes tambourine emphatically and SOUND CREW 1–5 shake rattles as HOUSE CHORUS raises hands to heads and shakes whole bodies.*)

STORYTELLER 1: Jack scurried into the oven.

(OVEN *forms and* SOUND CREW 2 *strikes wood block as* JACK *scurries.*)

STORYTELLER 2: In stomped the Giant, looking bigger and angrier than before.

GIANT *and* GIANT CHORUS (*making pounding motions with fists*): Fee, Fi, Fo, Fum, I smell the blood of an Englishman. Be he alive, or be he dead, I'll grind his bones to make my bread.

(SOUND CREW 5 *strikes drum on "Fee, Fi, Fo, Fum." SOUND CREW 4 scrapes guiro after "grind."*)

STORYTELLER 3: His wife said it was his imagination.

GIANT'S WIFE (*fidgeting*): It's only your imagination.

STORYTELLER 3: The Giant stomped to the table wanting breakfast now.

(SOUND CREW 5 *strikes bass drum for stomping to table.* TABLE *forms.*)

GIANT (*pounding fists*): Bring breakfast NOW.

(SOUND CREW 5 *strikes bass drum once for pounding.*)

STORYTELLER 4: His wife staggered in with a whole sheep and a five-gallon tub of juice.

(GIANT'S WIFE *mimes carrying a plate big enough to hold a sheep.*)

STORYTELLER 1: The Giant grabbed the sheep and ate it. He gulped the juice in two big glugs.

GIANT (*holding up huge tub*): Glug, glug.

STORYTELLER 2: He pounded for his magic hen.

(GIANT *mimes pounding* TABLE *with fist as* SOUND CREW 5 *hits bass drum once.*)

STORYTELLER 3: The Giant's Wife brought the hen to the table.

(GIANT'S WIFE *escorts* HEN *to* TABLE.)

STORYTELLER 4: The Giant demanded that the hen lay a golden egg.

GIANT (*roaring and pointing*): Lay a golden egg.

HEN (*raising wings*): Cackle.

(*SOUND CREW 2 strikes wood block. HEN lays golden egg. GIANT mimes holding up a small egg and examining it.*)

STORYTELLER 1: The Giant commanded a bigger one.

GIANT (*louder*): Lay a bigger one.

HEN (*raising wings higher, louder*): Cackle!

(*SOUND CREW 2 strikes wood block louder. HEN lays an egg the size of a child's football. GIANT mimes holding up the egg and examining it.*)

STORYTELLER 2: The Giant commanded a giant-sized golden egg.

GIANT: Lay a giant-sized golden egg.

HEN (*raising wings as high as possible, using loudest voice*): Cackle!

(*SOUND CREW 2 strikes wood block louder. GIANT mimes holding up the adult football-sized egg and examining it.*)

STORYTELLER 3: But again the Giant grew tired, and he fell to the floor, snoring in a stupor.

(*SOUND CREW 5 strikes drum as GIANT falls to floor. SOUND CREW 4 scrapes guiro for snoring.*)

STORYTELLER 4: And the whole house shook and trembled with the huge noise.

(*SOUND CREW 3 shakes tambourine and SOUND CREW 1–5 shake rattles. HOUSE CHORUS raises hands and shakes and trembles.*)

STORYTELLER 1: Jack tiptoed out of the oven. He tucked the hen under his arm.

(*SOUND CREW 2 strikes wood block for tiptoeing and tucking HEN under his arm.*)

STORYTELLER 2: But just as they were at the door, the hen let out a...

HEN: Cackle!

(*SOUND CREW 2 strikes wood block emphatically.*)

STORYTELLER 3: The Giant awoke and pounded for his hen.

(*GIANT sits up and pounds floor as SOUND CREW 5 strikes bass drum once.*)

Scene Eight

Characters Storytellers, Jack, Hen, Beanstalk, Clouds, Mother

STORYTELLER 4: Jack ran to the beanstalk and climbed down with the hen.

(*BEANSTALK and CLOUDS form. DOOR, OVEN, and TABLE sit in place. SOUND CREW 6 plays piano from high to low for climbing down. MOTHER takes position. BEANSTALK and CLOUDS sit in place once JACK climbs down.*)

STORYTELLER 1: He showed the hen to his mother, telling it to lay a golden egg.

JACK (*pointing proudly*): Lay a golden egg.

HEN (*raising wings*): Cackle.

> (SOUND CREW 2 *strikes wood block.* JACK *mimes handing small egg to* MOTHER.)

MOTHER (*holding up egg*): Wonderful.

JACK (*again pointing proudly*): Lay a bigger one.

HEN (*louder, raising wings higher*): Cackle!

> (SOUND CREW 2 *strikes wood block louder.* JACK *hands child's football-sized egg to* MOTHER.)

MOTHER (*holding egg higher*): Marvelous.

JACK (*pointing most proudly*): Lay a giant-sized golden egg.

HEN (*louder, wings raised as high as possible*): Cackle!

> (SOUND CREW 2 *strikes wood block louder.* JACK *hands adult football-sized egg to* MOTHER.)

MOTHER (*holding egg higher, enthusiastically*): Amazing!

STORYTELLER 2: But although the hen laid a golden egg every day, Jack wanted to try his luck once more.

STORYTELLER 3: So one morning before dawn, he jumped onto the beanstalk and climbed up.

> (BEANSTALK *and* CLOUDS *take position.* SOUND CREW 6 *strikes piano notes from low to high for climbing.*)

STORYTELLER 4: Again he hopped the clouds.

> (SOUND CREW 1 *rings wind chimes and* SOUND CREW 2 *and* SOUND CREW 4 *ring small hand bells.*)

STORYTELLER 1: Again he walked the dusty road.

> (SOUND CREW 1–5 *shake rattles.* BEANSTALK *and* CLOUDS *sit in place.*)

STORYTELLER 2: But he did not speak to the Giant's Wife.

Scene Nine

Characters Storytellers, Jack, Berry Bushes, Well, Door to Giant's House, Table, Broom Closet, Giant's Wife, Giant, Oven, Table, Harp, Beanstalk, Earth, Hen, Mother

STORYTELLER 3: He hid behind some berry bushes.

> (BERRY BUSHES *form and* JACK *hides behind them.*)

STORYTELLER 4: Until the Giant's Wife came out to the well and cranked up a pail of water.

> (WELL *forms.* GIANT'S WIFE *enters and* SOUND CREW 4 *scrapes guiro for cranking.*)

Developing Scripts for Myths and Tales

STORYTELLER 1: Then Jack sneaked inside the house and got into a broom closet.

(DOOR *and* BROOM CLOSET *form.* JACK *enters house.* SOUND CREW 4 *scrapes guiro as* JACK *opens squeaky door of* CLOSET.)

STORYTELLER 2: Immediately he heard thump, thump, thump.

(SOUND CREW 5 *strikes drum.*)

STORYTELLER 3: And the whole house began to shake and tremble.

(SOUND CREW 3 *shakes tambourine and* SOUND CREW 1–5 *shake rattles.* HOUSE CHORUS *raises hands and shakes and trembles.*)

STORYTELLER 4: In came the roaring Giant followed by his nervous wife.

GIANT *and* GIANT CHORUS (*bellowing and pounding*): Fee, Fi, Fo, Fum. I smell the blood of an Englishman. Be he alive, or be head dead, I'll grind his bones to make my bread.

STORYTELLER 1: The Giant's Wife glared at the oven.

(OVEN *forms.*)

GIANT'S WIFE (*pointing*): Check the oven.

STORYTELLER 2: The Giant did, but Jack wasn't there.

(GIANT *opens* OVEN DOOR, *looks inside, and slams door shut.* SOUND CREW 2 *strikes wood block emphatically for* OVEN *door slamming.*)

STORYTELLER 3: The Giant stomped to the table and pounded for breakfast.

(TABLE *forms.* GIANT *pounds* TABLE *as* SOUND CREW 5 *strikes bass drum once.*)

STORYTELLER 4: His wife staggered in with a cow and a 30-gallon drum of milk.

(GIANT'S WIFE *mimes carrying a tray big enough for a cow.*)

STORYTELLER 1: The Giant picked up the cow and ate it ravenously.

(GIANT *mimes eating.*)

STORYTELLER 1: He gulped the milk in one huge swallow.

GIANT (*drinking*): Glug.

STORYTELLER 2: He pounded for his golden harp.

(GIANT *pounds* TABLE *as* SOUND CREW 5 *strikes bass drum once.*)

STORYTELLER 3: The Giant's Wife rushed to the table with the harp.

(GIANT'S WIFE *escorts* HARP *to* TABLE.)

STORYTELLER 4: He pounded for the harp to sing.

GIANT (*roaring*): Harp, sing.

(SOUND CREW 1 *dings triangle as* HARP *in profile strikes a dramatic pose, one hand in the air.*)

HARP (*singing*): Lah-dah.

(SOUND CREW 6 *sweeps glissando along high piano notes for singing.*)

GIANT (*louder*): Sing again.

HARP (*posing in opposite direction*): Lah-dah.

(SOUND CREW 6 *sweeps a piano glissando.*)

STORYTELLER 1: Soon the Giant grew tired, his head nodded, and he fell to the floor, snoring in a stupor.

(SOUND CREW 5 *strikes drum as* GIANT *slumps to floor.* SOUND CREW 4 *scrapes guiro for snoring.*)

STORYTELLER 2: The whole house began to shake and tremble with the huge noise.

(SOUND CREW 3 *shakes tambourine and* SOUND CREW 1–5 *shake rattles.* HOUSE CHORUS *raises hands and shakes and trembles.*)

STORYTELLER 2: Jack opened the broom closet.

(SOUND CREW 4 *scrapes guiro as* JACK *cautiously opens* BROOM CLOSET *door.*)

STORYTELLER 3: He crept by the Giant and grabbed the harp.

(SOUND CREW 2 *strikes wood block for creeping.*)

STORYTELLER 4: But at the door, the harp called...

HARP (*musically*): Master.

(SOUND CREW 6 *sweeps glissando on high piano notes.*)

STORYTELLER 4: The Giant awoke and ran for Jack.

(SOUND CREW 6 *strikes low piano notes for running.* JACK *and* GIANT *exit kitchen through* DOOR, *and* DOOR *sits.*)

STORYTELLER 1: Clouds slowed the Giant.

(CLOUDS *encircle* GIANT *running in place.*)

STORYTELLER 2: Jack swung onto the beanstalk and climbed down.

(BEANSTALK *forms and* SOUND CREW 6 *strikes piano notes from high to low for climbing down.*)

STORYTELLER 3: But the Harp called...

HARP (*musically*): Master.

(SOUND CREW 6 *sweeps glissando.*)

STORYTELLER 4: The Giant jumped on the beanstalk.

Developing Scripts for Myths and Tales

Jack and the Beanstalk

STORYTELLER 1: When he reached the ground, Jack got an ax and chopped at the beanstalk. The Giant fell.

(SOUND CREW 2 *strikes wood block twice for chopping.* SOUND CREW 3 *shakes tambourine energetically, slapping it in the center emphatically for falling.*)

STORYTELLER 2: The Giant broke through the ground and disappeared under the earth.

(SOUND CREW 5 *strikes bass drum;* GIANT *freezes as* EARTH *places cloth over him;* SOUND CREW 5 *strikes drum again.*)

STORYTELLER 3: Jack proudly proclaimed the Giant's end.

JACK (*proudly, pointing*): That's the end of him.

STORYTELLER 4: His Mother was proud, too.

MOTHER (*putting a hand on Jack's shoulder*): I'm so proud.

STORYTELLER 1: And so, with the hen that laid golden eggs...

HEN (*coming between* JACK *and* MOTHER): Cackle!

(SOUND CREW 2 *strikes wood block as* HEN *lays football-sized egg;* JACK *examines it and smiles.*)

STORYTELLER 2: And the harp that sang...

HARP (*going next to* HEN, *gazing at* JACK *adoringly*): Master.

(SOUND CREW 6 *sweeps glissando on high piano notes.*)

STORYTELLER 3: Jack and his mother lived happily ever after.

(JACK, MOTHER, HEN, *and* HARP *bow and sit.*)

STORYTELLER 1 (*gesturing to departing characters*):

That's our tale from England's merry land,

A place of theatre, old and grand.

Now to keep you merry, too,

We'll dance our dance once more for you.

(STORYTELLER 1 *gestures to lead dancer, who moves to stage center, raising bells and waiting for taped music. The dancers dance as before, returning to their seats as* SOUND CREW 1 *fades out music.*)

Developing Scripts for Myths and Tales

Finale

STORYTELLER 1: Thank you students, adults, too.

STORYTELLER 2: For watching so kindly our show for you.

STORYTELLER 3: Of a British folk tale, old yet new.

STORYTELLER 4: We hope it came alive for you.

STORYTELLER 1: And here's a last tip from us, your friends.

STORYTELLER 2 (*holding up version of Jack and the Beanstalk*): Read a book of this story from beginning to end.

STORYTELLER 3: And study different cultures wherever they may be.

STORYTELLER 4: For the more that you know, the more you'll be...

(STORYTELLERS *gesture to all performers.*)

EVERYONE (*making big circular gesture around their heads*): Free!

STORYTELLER 1: The actors are...

STORYTELLER 2: The Sound Crew is...

STORYTELLER 3: The Storytellers are...

STORYTELLER 4: Thank you.

To end the performance, STORYTELLERS *1–4 introduce the performers, having them stand and say their names loudly and clearly. When all are standing,* STORYTELLERS *1–4 turn toward them and raise arms. Everyone follows, raising their arms and bringing them down together for a group bow, saying "Thank you" as they do so. Performers then sit for the audience performance discussion.*

Story Questions and Research Topics

To spark students' interest and enrich the cultural experience, provide a variety of materials for investigation, dramatic play, study, and observation. Suggestions include artifacts, clothing, utensils, photographs, artwork, and books. Discussion questions and research topics can be pursued before embarking on a drama experience, during play rehearsal, or after the production to support the culture being introduced.

Story Questions

1. What do you think is the most magical thing that happens in *Jack and the Beanstalk?* What is the funniest thing that happens? What is the scariest part of the story?

2. Who is your favorite character in the story and why?

3. Why did Jack sell the cow for beans? Do you think Jack's mother was right to be angry with Jack? Would you have sold the cow for beans? Explain your answer.

4. Why did Jack climb the beanstalk? What do you think he expected to find at the top?

5. What do you think caused the Giant to become such a bully?

6. What seemingly impossible tasks did Jack accomplish? Do you think Jack is a hero? Was Jack wrong to steal from the Giant? Explain your answer.

7. How is Jack different at the end of the story from how he was in the beginning? Jack might be called a trickster. A trickster is someone who uses tricks to defeat the enemy or to get something. In what ways is Jack a trickster?

Theater-Performance Questions

1. A *farce* is a comedy with broad humor, lots of surprises, and plenty of action. Could *Jack and the Beanstalk* be called a farce? Explain your reasoning with examples from the play.

2. A good way for an actor to become a character is to think of how that character looks. Choose a partner and describe to each other how the Giant in *Jack in the Beanstalk* looks—his hair, eyes, nose, mouth, teeth, arms, legs, and feet. Use your partner's description to draw a picture. You may also wish to find pictures in different versions of *Jack in the Beanstalk* and share them with the class. Repeat the exercise with other characters in the play.

3. Find out why Britain is noted for its excellent theatre and great actors. What training do actors in Britain receive?

Research Topics

1. What are some of the elements of a fairy tale? What is it about fairy tales that makes them so enjoyable? Read a fairy tale that you have never heard of before. Then use your own words to tell the story to the class. Try to express the feelings and traits of each character.

2. The Brothers Grimm are famous for their collections of folk and fairy tales. Read one that has always been one of your favorites. Do you like the way it was written? In what way was the story different from how you remembered it? What was your favorite part?

3. In *Gulliver's Travels* by Jonathan Swift, Gulliver visits the land of the Brobdingnags, who are giants. Read that episode in *Gulliver's Travels*. What are the giants like? How is Gulliver treated by the Giants?

4. Many myths feature giants as the first race of people to inhabit the earth. Read some of the stories from Scandinavia and other countries. How do the giants get along with the gods?

5. The name *Jack* is used in many stories and nursery rhymes. Find other stories and rhymes that have a character named Jack.

6. Find stories from other cultures in which a hero overcomes a giant or other monster. What does the hero do? What is the most difficult or suspenseful part of the story?

7. Find stories from other cultures in which a character goes off on an adventure alone. How is a story more exciting and dramatic when the character is alone rather than with a partner or group?

8. The trickster hero who tries to get something by tricking someone is popular in many cultures. Read and share stories of tricksters from other cultures, including African, Native North American Indian, and Hispanic.

Selected Bibliography
Versions of "Jack and the Beanstalk"

Briggs, Raymond. *Jim and the Beanstalk.* New York: Coward-McCann, 1970. Broadly comic sequel to the story.

De Regniers, Beatrice Schenk. *Jack and the Beanstalk, Retold in Verse.* Illustrated by Anne Wilsdorf. New York: Atheneum, 1985. Amusing retelling and pictures in verse. Students will enjoy seeing this alternative way of adapting a folk tale.

Galdone, Paul. *Jack and the Beanstalk.* New York: Clarion Books, 1974. A lively verse adaptation using an 1807 version of the story.

Paulson, Tim. *Jack and the Beanstalk and The Beanstalk Incident.* Illustrated by Mark Corcoran. New York: Carol Publishing Group, 1990. This version of the tale is told from the Giant's point of view.

Pearson, Susan. *Jack and the Beanstalk.* Illustrated by James Warhola. New York: Simon and Schuster, 1989. Vibrantly illustrated, evoking the supernatural elements of the tale. Excellent for students age nine and older to read and act.

Ross, Tony. *Jack and the Beanstalk.* New York: Delacorte Press, 1980. Comic spoof of the tale with vibrant, amusing illustrations that appeal to students age eight and older.

Giant Books

Dahl, Roald. *The BFG*. Illustrated by Quentin Blake. New York: Farrar, Straus, and Giroux, 1982. The Big Friendly Giant kidnaps Sophie from an orphanage, and they go to Giantland. For students age ten and older.

De Regniers, Beatrice Schenk. *Jack the Giant Killer*. Illustrated by Anne Wilsdorf. New York: Atheneum, 1987. Story in verse of another brave Jack who boldly defeats the wicked giant. Includes a section on "useful information about giants," helpful to actors depicting this role.

Manning-Sanders, Ruth. *The Book of Giants*. Illustrated by Robin Jacques. New York: E.P. Dutton, 1963. Giant stories from Georgia, Jutland, Germany, Norway, and Ireland, including *Jack and the Beanstalk* and several other *Jack the Giant Killer* stories. For students age ten and older.

Mayne, William, ed. *William Mayne's Book of Giants*. Illustrated by Raymond Briggs. New York: E.P. Dutton, 1969. Stories of giants of different cultures, including America, Norway, the Pacific Islands, Ireland, and Britain. Includes versions of *Jack and the Beanstalk*. For students age ten and older.

Swift, Jonathan. *Gulliver's Travels to Lilliput and Brobdingnag*. Illustrated by R.G. Mossa. London: Lamboll House, 1986. Large type and evocative illustrations make this a good version for older students.

Wilde, Oscar. *The Selfish Giant*. Illustrated by Lisbeth Zwerger. Saxonville, MA: Picture Book Studio USA, 1984. Dreamy pictures evoke the magical, classic tale of a giant who reforms.

Folk and Fairy Tale Collections

Ehrlich, Amy. *The Random House Book of Fairy Tales*. Illustrated by Diane Goode. New York: Random House, 1985. Favorite European folk tales, including *Sleeping Beauty, Beauty and the Beast, Jack and the Beanstalk,* and *Cinderella.*

Grimm, Jacob and Wilhelm. *Grimm's Fairy Tales*. Illustrated by Fritz Kredel. New York: Grosset and Dunlap, 1986. Reissue of a popular edition of the best-known tales along with some lesser-known tales.

Opie, Iona, and Peter Opie, eds. *The Classic Fairy Tales: New Edition*. New York: Oxford University Press, 1992. Twenty-four classic fairy tales in their original form edited by experts and accompanied by color and black-and-white illustrations.

Oxenbury, Helen. *The Helen Oxenbury Nursery Story Book*. New York: Alfred A. Knopf, 1985. Vividly illustrated collection of simple folk tales, such as *The Gingerbread Boy* and *Henny-Penny*. Good for older students to dramatize for younger students. Pictures will inspire them to act.

Swortzell, Lowell, ed. *All the World's a Stage, Modern Plays for Young People*. New York: Delacorte Press, 1972. Twenty-one great modern plays from around the world written to be performed for young people. For students age twelve and older.

CHAPTER TEN

Writing a Narrative Mime Script

Your choice of myths and tales to act are not limited to the scripts presented in this book. Many folk tales and myths can be adapted into plays that can be performed by students of all ages. In fact, students enjoy being involved in the adaptation process—from choosing the tale to writing the script—and the process is a valuable learning experience for all involved.

Use the following techniques to help students adapt any tale into a narrative mime script.

- Choose simple picture books that have action words or strong verbs in almost every sentence. Even for older students, picture books are a good starting point since they break down a story into manageable bits of information.
- The essence of a narrative mime script is action. Help students identify action moments in the story chosen. If a sentence has no action, change it or eliminate it. For example, "Once upon a time there were three bears" might be changed to "One morning, Mother Bear got out of bed and stretched and yawned. She called Papa and Baby Bear."
- Eliminate nonessential words to pare down the script to its most basic action. For example, "the dog trotted briskly" is not necessary; "the dog trotted" is enough.
- Use vivid verbs. "Spied," "peered," "scowled," "glared," or "squinted," are clearer and easier to act than "looked."
- Try to have storytellers' lines give characters cues for what to say:

    STORYTELLER 1: The Chief commanded them to obey.

    CHIEF: I command you to obey.

    Students can also improvise their own dialogue using the storytellers' cues:

    STORYTELLER 1: The Chief commanded them to obey.

    CHIEF: You must obey me!

- Include customs or speech of the culture. Study customs depicted in pictures from the storybook and/or other resources, follow the story's style, and perhaps consult other books describing cultural rituals and customs.

- Decide where to incorporate sound effects to enhance the acting and reinforce established themes.
- Include roles for animals and inanimate objects.
- Use as many characters as necessary; some students can play more than one part and certain parts can be played by two or more students.
- Use at least one storyteller and not more than four.

Working in Groups

It is not necessary for the teacher to be the sole author of the narrative mime script. Students are often the most appropriate authors (since they will be acting the roles), and the process of script-writing is a valuable learning experience. The following techniques can be used to organize students in groups in order to write their own narrative mime script to act.

- Choose a picture book for students to dramatize (or have students choose the book). Read it aloud, showing the class the pictures.
- Help students list the characters needed to act the story.
- Work with students to divide the story into scenes, breaking down the action of the story into small segments.
- Divide the class into groups, one for each scene. Have each group choose a secretary. Students in each group work together to develop storyteller narration and character dialogue for their scene. (Alternatively, each group can work on the play as a whole, and can compare their version of the whole play to that of the other groups.) The secretary records the information in script form. Students then add sound effects and possibly add more object parts to the script, as necessary.
- Students practice acting the story in their groups, testing for what works and what does not. They might decide on sound effects as they go along. If there are not enough instruments to use with every group, encourage students to improvise using objects around the room.
- Students share their performances with the class. The class comments, first mentioning what was good about the performance and then suggesting additions that will improve it.
- Students comment on any script adaptations that are necessary to create smooth transitions from one group's scene to the next, if appropriate. This way, scenes will flow smoothly from one into another and it will not be obvious that more than one group authored the script. If individual groups are developing the whole play, this step is unnecessary.
- Students return to their groups and run through their scenes again, incorporating the suggestions.
- Again students share their performances with the class and any final necessary adaptations are made. The teacher can then proceed to auditioning for roles.

PART THREE

Appendix

Bibliography

In addition to the selected bibliographical information provided with each play, the following books can provide useful resource material to enhance the learning experience for students and teachers alike. Books are listed according to category for ease of use.

Creative Drama and Acting

Blackaby, Susan. *Quick and Easy Holiday Skits.* Mahwah, NJ: Troll Associates, 1992. Puppet shows, choral readings, readers theatre, and plays for all ages and all occasions.

Cook, Wayne. *Center Stage. A Curriculum for the Performing Arts.* Menlo Park, CA: Dale Seymour Publications, 1993. This two-volume curriculum provides valuable information for both drama specialists and classroom teachers. One volume is for kindergarten through grade three and a second covers grades four through six. Thirty sequential lessons of creative drama activities for each grade level. Upper grade volume has background and activities for putting on a play.

Lewis, Mary Kane. *Acting for Children: A Primer.* New York: The John Day Company, 1969. Includes acting and speech activities and teaches students how to block a play and direct improvisations, pantomimes, and plays.

Malkin, Michael R. *Training the Young Actor.* New York: A. S. Barnes and Co., Inc., 1979. Methods and hands-on activities to train students ages seven to twelve to act in plays and perform puppetry and readers theatre.

McGaw, Charles J., and Gary Blake. *Acting is Believing: A Basic Method.* New York: Holt, Rinehart and Winston, Inc., 1986. An excellent acting text explaining the actor's craft for high school students and older. Activities could be adapted for younger students.

Novelly, Maria C. *Theatre Games for Young Performers: Improvisations & Exercises for Developing Acting Skills.* Colorado Springs, CO: Merriwether Publishing Ltd., 1985. Acting activities in mime, voice, improvisation, and scene building, with techniques for planning a drama program.

Scher, Anna, and Charles Verrall. 200+ *Ideas for Drama*. Portsmouth, NH: Heinemann Educational Books, 1992. A recipe book with acting activities, many of which can be done on the spot. Suggestions for simple and more complex productions are included.

Schwartz, Dorothy, and Dorothy Aldrich, ed. *Give Them Roots...And Wings!* New Orleans, LA: Anchorage Press, 1985. Classroom-tested activities from simple to complex and theory by experts, with a final chapter on dramatizing stories.

Siks, Geraldine Brain. *Drama with Children*. Second Edition. New York: Harper & Row, 1983. Helpful, goal-oriented, creative dramatics and a chapter on playmaking.

Spolin, Viola. *Improvisation for the Theatre: A Handbook of Teaching and Directing Techniques*. Chicago: Northwestern University Press, 1983. Widely used text with activities for training students age ten and older to act with authenticity.

Thistle, Louise. *Dramatizing Aesop's Fables*. Menlo Park, CA: Dale Seymour Publications, 1993. Techniques and acting activities for acting Aesop's fables in the classroom. Prepares students for putting on a formal play. Acting activities, sound effect and costume suggestions, and art and critical thinking questions are included for each fable.

Creating Simple Costumes

Berk, Barbara, and Jeanne Bendick. *The First Book of Stage Costume and Make-Up*. New York: Franklin Watts, 1954. Describes with inviting illustrations how to create simple costumes of all types, using things found around the house.

Chernoff, Goldie Taub. *Easy Costumes You Don't Have to Sew*. Illustrated by Margaret A. Hartelius. New York: Four Winds Press, 1975. Original ideas for simple costumes that can be made almost immediately, including paper bag hats and plastic garbage bag tunics.

Cummings, Richard. *101 Costumes For All Ages, All Occasions*. Boston: Plays, Inc., 1987. Inspiring and cleverly illustrated suggestions for how to adapt clothes and make simple costumes for all cultures and historical time frames. Older students might get ideas for making their own costumes.

Dazian Theatrical Fabrics and Supplies, 2014 Commerce Street, Dallas, TX, 75201 (214-748-8543). Catalogue includes samples of striking fabrics and simple costume pieces, including many styles of hats that are reasonably priced.

Hailey, Gail E. *Costumes for Plays and Playing*. New York: Methuen, 1978. Describes how to make all types of costumes and costume pieces, including animal head-pieces and tails, and how to adapt clothes, hats, and fabrics into costumes.

Rubie's Costume Company, One Rubie Plaza, Richmond Hill, NY, 11418 (718-846-1008). An inspiring catalogue with helpful ideas and almost every type of costume to rent or buy, including pages and pages of hats.

Making Musical Instruments and Sound Effects

Newman, Frederick R. *Mouthsounds.* New York: Workman, 1980. Amusingly illustrates how to vocally create animal sounds, musical instruments, and noises such as ping-pong pops and the telephone dial. Includes a record with some of the sounds. Appealing to students age ten and older.

West Music Company, 1208 5th Street, Coralville, IA, 52241 (1-800-397-9378). A very complete catalogue of reasonably priced rhythm instruments from many cultures. Also has books describing the Orff Schulwerk system of teaching music, which is an approach used in this book.

Wiseman, Ann. *Making Musical Things.* New York: Charles Scribner's Sons, 1979. Simple, inventive instruments made of kitchen utensils, pieces of wood, pipe, and other ordinary things.

Stories and Storytelling

Carpenter, Humphrey, and Mari Prichard. *The Oxford Companion to Children's Literature.* New York: Oxford University Press, 1984. About 2000 entries including information on individual works, authors, genres, characters, countries and regions, and illustration. Invaluable resource for teachers of older and gifted students.

Clarkson, Atelia, and Gilbert B. Cross. *World Folktales: A Scribner Resource Collection.* New York: Charles Scribner's Sons, 1980. Over sixty folk tales from around the world, with notes on each and a section on ways to integrate them into the curriculum.

Pellowski, Anne. *The Family Storytelling Handbook: How to Use Stories, Anecdotes, Rhymes, Handkerchiefs, Paper and Other Objects to Enrich Your Family Traditions.* Illustrated by Lynn Sweat. New York: Macmillian, Inc., 1987. An expert in children's storytelling and world cultures gives the purposes of storytelling and illustrates intriguing ways to tell stories for anyone age nine and above.

————. *The Story-Vine: A Source Book of Unusual and Easy-to-Tell Stories from Around the World.* Illustrated by Lynn Sweat. New York: Macmillan, Inc., 1984. Describes telling stories with string, pictures, sand, dolls, riddles, and music, as is done in various cultures. Fascinating and practical for age nine and older.

Multicultural Resources

Allen, Judy, Earldene McNeill and Velma Schmidt. *Cultural Awareness for Children.* Reading, MA: Addison-Wesley Publishing Company, 1992. Stimulating activities and information on several of the cultures depicted in this book.

Blackaby, Susan. *One World: Multicultural Projects and Activities.* Mahwah, NJ: Troll Associates, 1992. Activities and group projects are linked to folk tales, oral history, and contemporary fiction for each culture.

Miller-Lachmann, Lyn. *Our Family Our Friends: An Annotated Guide to Significant Multicultural Books for Children and Teenagers.* New Providence, NJ: R. R. Bowker, 1992. Covers multicultural literature worldwide, broken down into countries and arranged by grade level—pre-school through high school.

Schon, Isabel. *A Bicultural Heritage: Themes for the Exploration of Mexican and Mexican-American Culture in Books for Children and Adolescents.* Metuchen, NJ: Scarecrow Press, 1978. Uses five books to describes how to increase students' understanding of the customs, folklore, and history of Mexican and Mexican-American culture.

———. *A Hispanic Heritage: A Guide to Juvenile Books About Hispanic People and Cultures,* (3 vols.). Metuchen, NJ: Scarecrow Press, 1980, 1985, and 1988. A three-volume collection evaluating books about Latin America and Hispanic Americans. Highly recommended books are starred.

Slapin, Beverly, and Doris Seale. *Through Indian Eyes: The Native Experience in Books for Children.* Philadelphia, PA: New Society, 1991. Reviews over 100 books with Native American Indian topics from an American Indian perspective.

Woodland Pattern Book Center, 720 E. Locust Street, Milwaukee, WI, 53212 (414-263-5001). Excellent catalogues of books on Hispanic, black, Native American, and Asian subjects and themes.

Directing a Play

Allensworth, Carl. *The Complete Play Production Handbook,* revised edition. New York: Harper and Row, 1982. Excellent, clear, complete guide to the fundamentals of theatre and directing a play.

Dale Seymour Publications, 200 Middlefield Road, Menlo Park, CA, 94025 (800-872-1100). Publishes a *Classroom Posters* catalogue, an excellent source of images to use for inspiration and to create atmosphere.

Davis, Jed, and Mary Jane Evans. *Theatre for Children and Youth.* New Orleans, LA: Anchorage Press, 1982. Covers all major areas of the subject.

Latham, Jean Lee. *Do's and Don'ts of Drama.* Woodstock, IL: The Dramatic Publishing Company, 1935. Still in print because of its succinct and sometimes humorous practical tips on play direction.

Rosenberg, Helane S., and Christine Prendergast. *Theatre For Young People: A Sense of Occasion.* New York: Holt, Rinehart and Winston, 1983. Describes how to direct adults (high school and above) in plays for young people, but has valuable directing tips for anyone interested in play direction.

Ross, Beverly B., and Jean P. Durgin. *Junior Broadway: How to Produce Musicals with Children 9 to 13.* Jefferson, NC: McFarland and Company, 1983. A practical guide by authors who have been through the process.

Readers Theatre

Bauer, Caroline Feller. *Presenting Readers Theatre.* New York: H. W. Wilson Co., 1987. Lively plays and poems that will appeal to children. Clearly discusses how to perform readers theatre in the classroom.

Hansen, Merrily P. *Now Presenting: Classic Tales for Readers Theatre.* Menlo Park, CA: Addison-Wesley Publishing Company, 1992. Illustrated scripts for six plays accompanied by teaching suggestions, simple costume patterns, and ideas for props.

Dance and Celebrations

Ancona, George. *Dancing Is.* New York: E.P. Dutton, 1981. Describes how dance means different things at different times and for different cultures. Illustrated with drawings and photos of dance celebrations in many parts of the world, including Africa and Mexico.

Van Straalen, Alice. *The Book of Holidays Around the World.* New York: E.P. Dutton, 1986. Beautifully illustrated with color reproductions from children's books and photographs of actual celebrations, including Ghana's Yam Festival and Guatemala's Sealing the Frost festival. Valuable for age eight and older.

Weikart, Phyllis S. *Teaching Movement and Dance: A Sequential Approach to Rhythmic Movement*, 3rd ed. Ypsilanti, MI: High Scope, 1989. Instructions for teaching approximately 110 beginning folk dances. Includes tape cassettes of music for the dances.